# BITS AND PIECES

## A COLLAGE OF MY BITSIAN MEMORIES

HARSHITA NANDA

Copyright © Harshita Nanda
All Rights Reserved.

This book has been published with all efforts taken to make the material error-free after the consent of the author. However, the author and the publisher do not assume and hereby disclaim any liability to any party for any loss, damage, or disruption caused by errors or omissions, whether such errors or omissions result from negligence, accident, or any other cause.

While every effort has been made to avoid any mistake or omission, this publication is being sold on the condition and understanding that neither the author nor the publishers or printers would be liable in any manner to any person by reason of any mistake or omission in this publication or for any action taken or omitted to be taken or advice rendered or accepted on the basis of this work. For any defect in printing or binding the publishers will be liable only to replace the defective copy by another copy of this work then available.

*Dedicated to my alma mater, BITS Pilani. My life would have been very different if I had not been a student there!*

# Contents

# Contents

# Acknowledgements

I owe a debt of gratitude to all my readers who have constantly encouraged and motivated me with their constant support.

I am grateful to Dr K.K. Singh and Dr Neeru Sood for their kindness in writing the foreword. Girija Hariharan, thank you so much for translating my words into illustrations. Aarthi Bharat for fact-checking when my memory was not so reliable. Special mention to the team of the 1996 BITS Pilani yearbook, which was a veritable font of ideas.

It would be remiss of me not to acknowledge the people who have been my pillars of strength. My parents, Dr S. K. Nanda and Mrs Vinod Nanda, and my sisters, Chhavi and Aditi. My sons, Kush and Rishabh, who unknowingly, motivate me to do my best.

My husband Ashish has always been my North Star. **BITS and Pieces** would not have existed without his help, guidance and support. I am so grateful that you are always by my side.

# Foreword

BITS Pilani was where I met Harshita in my MSc Physics class for the first time. This bubbly girl was full of energy and had sparkles in her eyes. Five years of stay at BITS groomed her to not only become an Electrical and Electronics Engineer and a Physics graduate, but also a passionate reader and a skilled writer.

It was a pleasant surprise when we reconnected with Harshita and Ashish again in Dubai. From a professor-student relationship, our relationship evolved, to us becoming a family. Her love for English literature in the meantime had grown and was visible on the bookshelves of her house in Dubai.

It was sometime during the first week of November 2020, that she sent a link to one of her first stories. It was then we got to know how beautifully she could pen down her emotions in a simple yet effective way. Though initially, Harshita started pouring her words through blogs, in 2021, she took a step forward by publishing her first book, "Xanadu: Three Souls Searching for Their Paradise".

Today what you have in your hand is the fruit of that sapling which she was nourished for so many years with nutrients of her thoughts, time & hard work.

The very first edition of "**BITS and Pieces: A Collage Of My BITSian Memories**" narrates Harshita's journey in BITS from different perspectives and dimensions of life, starting from a young girl who joins a new campus, her attachments with BITS and places on campus, her journey with classmates and professors, rising in love (not falling), gossiping with friends, going through ups and downs of examination, make-ups, CGPA, practice school (internship) and most importantly, passion for reading.

This book holds a special place for BITS Pilani alumnus and staff or anyone who has had the opportunity to be associated with BITSPilani, as it serves as a trip down memory lane filled with nostalgia. For newcomers, this book will help them see the beauty of college life at a place like BITS Pilani.

Dr. K.K. Singh & Dr. Neeru Sood<br>Professors BITS Pilani, Dubai Campus

# Foreword

BITS Pilani is a private world for every one of its students with its very own sensorial memories and nostalgia for extremely specific things that only the student and the place hold for each other.

There are specific memories that are crystal clear for me. My favourite place on campus, a particular ED table in FD1 with cobwebs that I studied most afternoons. A specific brush from M17 that I used to carry in my bag that later became the name of my artistic journey, *2flatbrush*.

But though BITS may dwell differently within each of us, vanishing slowly as we age and drift apart, there is a common emotion and language of BITSians all over.

Through Harshita's book, "**BITS and Pieces: A Collage Of My BITSian Memories**", and her recollections, we identify and remind ourselves of this wonderful world that we once inhabited and forever carry in our hearts.

It was a pleasure illustrating her BITS and bits of my BITS, through this wonderful book.

Girija Hariharan @2flatbrush

# Author's Note

In August 1997, a bespectacled, nerdy young girl got off from a jeep at the Pilani bus stand. She had travelled from Chennai to New Delhi and then on the metre gauge train from Delhi to get off at Loharu. A jeep was hired from Loharu for the final leg of the journey to Pilani. Accompanied by her father, she had a suitcase, a steel trunk and a bister band ( a bedroll having a mattress, a quilt and a pillow). As she entered the campus through imposing gates, her heart quaked. But outwardly, she seemed calm, her shoulders squared. She had mentally determined that she was going to have fun and avoid hiding in the shadows, as she had done before. That campus would be her home for the next four years.

Dear reader, that young eighteen-year-old was me. It may sound like a cliche, but it feels like time has flown by in the blink of an eye. In August 2022, it would be twenty-five years since I first stepped into the campus of my college, BITS Pilani.

The idea for the book came when I wrote three blog posts on an online platform about my college days. Writing those posts made me realise how much we miss those days and how many of us count our college days as the best years of our life. The days when we tiptoed into the adult world, learnt new responsibilities and yet had so much fun that they became a highlight of our lives.

For the book, "**BITS and Pieces: A Collage Of My BITSian Memories**", I have picked each alphabet, and written the corresponding BITSian word/slang and/or the emotion that word aroused. Part memoir, part glossary, this book is my humble tribute to my alma mater.

And also, a way to keep my memories of those halcyon days fresh.

Harshita Nanda
1997B5A3164

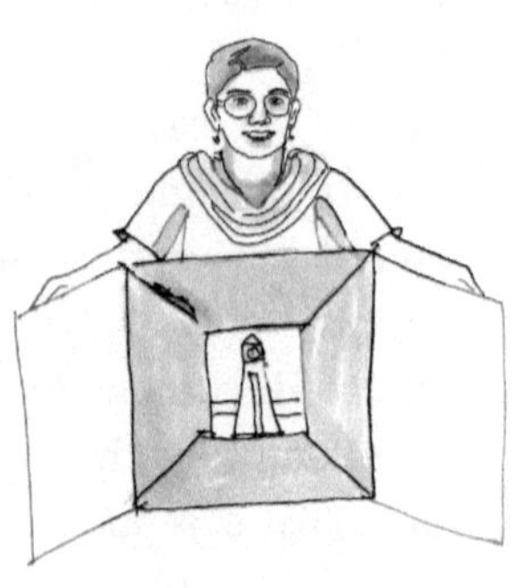

# CHAPTER ONE

# ADMISSION AND APOGEE

The best way to start anything is from the beginning. This is the story of how I became a student of BITS Pilani, one of the most prestigious colleges in the country.

Growing up in the small town of Dehradun, I was not aware of a college called BITS Pilani. In fact, when one of my school seniors got admission into BITS Pilani, I had no clue. All I understood was, that she was going to "some college in Rajasthan". You can blame my ignorance either on my disinterest or on the lack of awareness in a small town about the outside world in the early nineties. I did learn a little more about BITS Pilani after the family moved to Chennai. Yet, it was still not enough for me to be enthusiastic about applying since I was not interested in doing engineering. My older cousins and sister were in the medical field, and I had hoped to pursue the same.

I, however, was gently persuaded by my father to fill out the form for BITS Pilani. It was supposed to be a backup if I failed to clear my medical entrance exams. This turned out to be true. I failed to clear any of the medical entrances I had attempted. St. Stephens, New Delhi (where I secretly did want to study), was also ruled out (despite an interview call) since travelling from Chennai to New Delhi only for a college interview was not practically feasible.

With all my options reaching a dead end, I was resigned to doing an undergraduate course in a Chennai college. A college, whose atmosphere was stricter than my ex-school However, on the 6th of July, 1997, the postman dropped a letter in our letterbox. It was an acceptance letter from BITS Pilani, offering me a seat in MSc(Hons) Physics. Reading the letter, I was overjoyed. The letter was my ticket out of a college I hated attending. Thus, despite having almost zero knowledge about BITS Pilani (apart from the fact that it was in Rajasthan), I decided I was going to BITS Pilani. In those days, grade twelve marks were the only criteria for admission to BITS Pilani. This admission policy gave me a shot at doing a professional engineering course when most of the avenues were closed to me. For given my track record with entrance tests, I doubt I would have cleared their current entrance test, BITSAT.

Sometimes, when I look back at the past, I wonder what would have happened if I had insisted on going for the interview at St. Stephens. Not to sound immodest, but my grades (at least in those days) were good enough to get a seat.

But then, I look at my life, its course determined by my action of taking admission to BITS Pilani.

And I smile, for I would have it no other way.

3-day event held in March, A Professions-Oriented Gathering Over Educational Experience or APOGEE, is all about science, technology and everything technical. The various engineering and science departments would showcase their technologies/breakthroughs. The departments would put up models/displays/projects and try to outdo one another in showing the most innovative technical content. A nerd's delight, for three days, the talk would only be on which department's technical prowess outshone the others. While I did participate in APOGEE ( though not very enthusiastically) in the first three years, by my fourth year I had realised I was not very technically inclined. That year, I escaped to my uncle's house in Dehradun during the APOGEE week.

I recently checked the website of APOGEE, and all I can say is that APOGEE has certainly grown bigger and better than before.

I do think that a chapter on A will be incomplete without a mention of Audi and ANC.

Audi in BITS Pilani does not mean the German car brand. Instead, it means the Auditorium. The one-stop venue for orientations, fashion shows, Founder's Day events, movie nights, music nights, plays, rock shows, etc. Many evenings were spent perched on its wooden seats, creating everlasting memories. I even reached its backstage once when I was a part of the production team for a Hindi play.

ANC, aka All-Night Canteen, is something most BITSians would have fond memories of. As the name suggests, it was a place where the hunger pangs of students could be satisfied once the messes closed for the night. Unfortunately, I have non-existent memories and feelings for this place (I can imagine some of the BITSians reading the book, screeching in horror at this statement).

AUDI
APOGEE '98
ALL NIGHT CANTEEN

# CHAPTER TWO

# B5 By Choice And BSL

"B5 by choice?!" This question, asked by a shocked senior during ragging, followed me my entire BITSian life ( and even later). B5, in case you readers are wondering, is the code for the discipline MSc (Hons)Physics, the four-year integrated course I joined in BITS Pilani. My picking Physics as my first preference was surprising to people because my normalized rank (more about it in alphabet N) was 164. This meant that I could have gotten admission directly into one of the branches of engineering (though not Computer Science or EEE). People found it unfathomable that someone would pick an MSc course, and that also physics, as their first choice. Because you know, a B.E. degree in any branch is more valuable and better respected than a plain MSc degree.

How was I to explain, without appearing like a fool, that when I had filled the forms of BITS Pilani, my knowledge about BITS was practically zero? Also, when filling out the form for BITS Pilani, I was still banking on the fact that I might clear at least one of the medical entrances I had attempted. I had zero interest (or awareness) in doing an engineering course. Thus, while filling out the form, I did not even fill the B.E. courses as the options. I only applied for MSc!

My plan, if I failed to get into medicine, was to do MSc, followed by a PhD and become a lecturer (go figure)! Physics and Maths, being my favourite subjects in school, were my first two choices, followed by the other options for MSc. I, of course, had no clue at all about what I was getting myself into. Physics in college was very different and obviously, much more difficult than Physics in school.

But did the difficulty of Physics in college take away the love I had for physics?

No!

I discovered that Physics has a multi-faceted beauty that most people are oblivious about. True, some branches of Physics still give me nightmares when I think about them (Classical Mechanics, for example). But some, like electromagnetic theory and astrophysics, still entice me. Thanks to my knowledge of Physics, I could also (to some level) understand the movie Interstellar without having to resort to Google!

So yes, I still do proudly say that I am B5 by choice!

But was I the only one in my batch who had picked Physics without coercion or as a last resort? No, my fellow first-year roommate was also a fellow lunatic. She was also a B5 by choice with a normalized rank of 169! So yes, people like us, who enjoy physics, do exist.

One term with "B" that I will always associate with BITS Pilani is BSL. BITS Pilani had a robust Student's Union though it was strictly non-political. For the student union activities, there was a separate block, called the Student

Union Block or SUB. Amongst other clubs, it housed Jhankaar, the audio cassette library (more about it in alphabet J) and BSL, or BITS Student Library. BSL was the only library on campus that had fiction books.

I, a voracious reader, discovered BSL during my first year and became an eager member. By my second year, I became so involved in BSL that I, my fellow B5 by choice lunatic roommate and a few other friends became the ones responsible for its running and maintenance. We took turns in taking shifts in managing the library during its opening hours. The only time I attended the New Delhi Book Fair was for the purpose to buy books for BSL. We used to even clean the library ourselves (once even begging the boys in the hostel across the student union block for jhaddoo).

BSL had two dark, rather poky rooms. The inner room had steel racks full of books. This room always smelled musty with a peculiar old-book smell. A smell, that was familiar and dear for bookworms like me. This inner room could only be accessed from the outer room, which had a solid wood desk and chair, where we used to play pretend librarians. I wonder if that desk still exists and if it still has yellow paint splatters on the edges. The paint spatters were from the time when I took advantage of being a BSL volunteer and used the desk to make posters for the Hindi Press Club during Oasis2K.

One might wonder why I spent so much time and energy on BSL when it was purely voluntary. The reason was simple. I loved books and reading. BSL was the only way I could be close to books and work with them. Plus, being a volunteer meant I could take books for reading at my pleasure and time and not be restricted by the one book per turn rule!

BSL not only provided me with a place where I could indulge in my passion for reading, but it also played an important role in the initial days of my romance with hubby dearest!

Other terms starting with "B", that were an important part of BITSian life were, Basant Panchami (the founding day of BITS), BOSM (the BITS Sports meet held every September), and Bogs (the BITSian name for Bathrooms).

# CHAPTER THREE

# C'NOT, CYCLES AND CGPA

Our world in BITS Pilani was limited to our campus.

The BITS Pilani campus was sprawling 328 acres. It housed the academic blocks, the hostels, the temples, residential areas for faculty and other staff, and of course, the all-important C'not. C'not (pronounced similar to Connaught) was a short stretch of street, hardly half a kilometre in length, with stores on both sides. This included Gandhi Ashram, from where I used to buy khadi kurtas; Mittal stores, where we bought toiletries, gift items etc. You name it, Mittal stores had it; An audio cassette shop run by a father of a friend; An STD/PCO/courier place.

C'not was also the home of iconic BITS restaurants like Blue Moon, Annapoorna, Sharma and Volga. You talk to any BITSian, and they will smile at the memories of the food in these restaurants. Blue Moon's Maggi (paneer, masala, plain, fried) was legendary, and Chimpu Bhaiya, with his trusted blender, could whizz milkshakes in a jiffy. Despite having passed out from BITS Pilani years ago, I still try to replicate (and fail) the taste of Blue Moon's fried Maggi. Alas, Chimpu Bhaiya went to his happy hunting grounds a few years ago, and BITS Pilani lost an icon.

Sharma Restaurant served North Indian fare and used to be my favourite, as the owner of the restaurant was always so welcoming and fed us like family members. Annapoorna used to be popular for its dosas while the Volga was the priciest of the lot, serving firangi food like burgers/sandwiches(made desi style, of course). The Volga was the only one that offered a modicum of privacy and was thus slightly more popular with dating couples. These restaurants all had seating under the stars with their tables painted a bright sky blue.

C'not was where we BITSians hung out in the evenings, and I have many happy memories of the place. Memories of laughter, of gossip, of friendship, of togetherness. Of Birthday parties and parties to celebrate placements; Of the crowds there during Holi/Diwali dinner when the mess workers would be on a holiday; Of being caught having a dinner date in the Volga and being teased later; Of just hanging out when we needed a break either from studies or from the hostel food.

There is one memory of C'not that is etched in my mind. One evening, my friends and I were not in the mood to eat dinner in our hostel mess. However, quite a few of us were running low on cash, and we didn't have the money to splurge on a proper meal. We hit upon the brainwave to pool all the coins we had, coming up to a grand total of about 80 rupees. With that money, we purchased a loaf of bread and a plate of paneer Maggi from Blue Moon. And this simple dinner was sufficient to satisfy the hunger pangs of the five girls. It was one of the most enjoyable meals I had ever had. We laughed and giggled throughout the meal, proud to have hit on a novel way to save money and yet, have fun together.

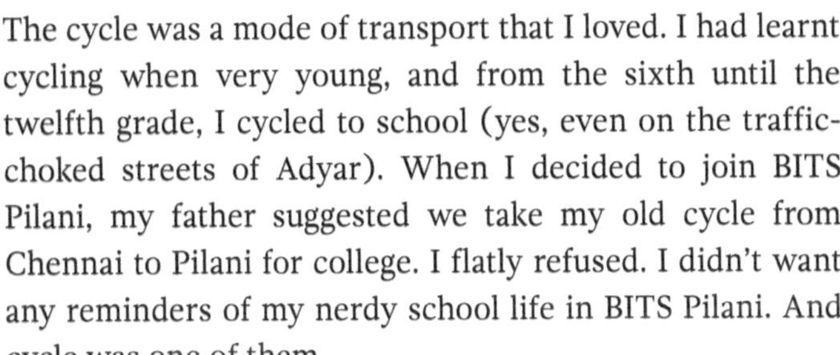

The cycle was a mode of transport that I loved. I had learnt cycling when very young, and from the sixth until the twelfth grade, I cycled to school (yes, even on the traffic-choked streets of Adyar). When I decided to join BITS Pilani, my father suggested we take my old cycle from Chennai to Pilani for college. I flatly refused. I didn't want any reminders of my nerdy school life in BITS Pilani. And cycle was one of them.

But, do you remember the fact that I knew zero about BITS Pilani? Little did I know what an integral part cycle was going to be in my BITSian life!

The cycle was the only mode of transportation in BITS Pilani. And this was true for everyone. In our days, all the BITSian girl students had one. Even highly respected professors would be seen sedately cycling down the tree-lined avenues. There were dedicated cycle parking stations in front of the academic blocks and hostels. One of the unspoken rules of cycles was that even if you left yours standing upright in the stand, it would usually be at the bottom of the cycle heap when you came back after a class. And then, you would hop impatiently, waiting for others to pick up their cycles before you could extricate yours.

I tried surviving without a cycle in my first year. But the daily walk to and fro between the academic block and hostel, and of course, the walks to BSL and C'not to hang out with friends, made me realise that my father was right and I was wrong.

I did need a cycle.

Now buying a new cycle was an expense I wanted to avoid. Especially when this expense could have been avoided if I had listened to my father in the first place! So,

I decided to buy one from a senior who was about to pass out for a princely sum of 250 rupees. The cycle had been silver when new, but when I bought it, the colour was a mix of grey and rust. It didn't have a carrier, and the break had an annoying tendency to jam at the wrong minute, making it (literally) jump in the air (usually with me in the saddle). Its stand was shaky, with a tendency to topple over at the slightest gust of wind. In other words, my new/old cycle was a decrepit heap.

But for the next three years, it was my trusted steed, carrying me to all corners of campus and once, even to Panchvati. On completing my four years, unwilling to foist it on an unsuspecting junior, I regretfully left the cycle to its own devices.

The last I saw my cycle in 2002, it was forlornly standing with its tyres deflated in front of a Meera Bhawan block, waiting for someone to claim it.

If you thought BITS Pilani was all about cycling down its tree-lined avenues and wolfing down Maggi at C'not, then you would only be partially right. BITS Pilani was also about CGPA. BITS Pilani was one of the first universities in India to adopt the American system of grading. For each course, the marks received by the students were plotted on a graph. The individual grade was then awarded according to the bell curve formed. The student's final grade and the credit of each course came together to form the grade point average(GPA) of a semester, with 10 being the highest. But the catch was that last term's GPA was also added to the current term's GPA. This was a student's CGPA or the Cumulative Grade Point Average. All the grades received by a student right from the first term were reflected in a student's CGPA. So yes, even if one scored a perfect "10" in the last term, the "D" one made in the first term, would come back to haunt, spoiling the perfect score. CGPA's importance was at the end of the first year when Dual Degree was awarded based on it. And then again in the last year, when the companies for which you could apply for placements were also determined by the CGPA.

CGPA was the bane of my existence. I could never recover from the slip and fall of my first year in BITS Pilani and managed to boost my CGPA only by doing two semesters of Practice School.

# CHAPTER FOUR

# DUAL DEGREES AND DAY SCHOLARS

"**D**" for "*Dhakkan*"! This was the first word that came to my mind for the alphabet "**D**" when I started planning out the A2Z of BITS Pilani. "Dhakan" was the BITSian slang for the grade "D", the one that would continue to haunt your CGPA till you passed out. Then I thought, why bore you, dear readers, with a grade that we all wished to escape (but one that did latch on to our CGPA's). So, the two terms that I picked for the alphabet "D" were Dual Degree and Day Scholar.

Dual Degree was one of the main charms for the popularity of BITS Pilani. BITS Pilani had two main streams, the engineering stream and the four years integrated MSc courses ( BPharm was also offered in BITS Pilani ). The MSc Courses were further divided into the regular MSc courses (Maths, Economics, Physics, Biological Sciences, Chemistry) and MSc Tech courses( Information Systems, Finance, Engineering Technology, General

Studies). Now, the main aim of students who came to BITS Pilani was to do engineering. So how could someone, who entered the college as an MSc student, do engineering?

Well, with the help of a Dual Degree.

After getting a toe-hold in BITS Pilani by taking admission in MScs, at the end of the first year, based on the CGPA, the student could apply for Dual. A dual degree meant that for an added year of study (five instead of the usual four), a student could do two-degree courses. MSc (that the student joined first) and Engineering (that the student was allotted after the first year). This was possible since in BITS Pilani, for the first two years all the students, irrespective of their discipline, had to do the same courses. Specialization happened from the third year onwards when Core Discipline Courses, called the CDCs, were introduced. So, a student with a dual would do their MSc CDCs in their third year and their dual CDCs in the fourth year (with their junior batch). They would pass out a year later than their friends who would have joined engineering.

Now coming to the fun part. Do you remember how I was B5 by choice since I was adamant about not doing Engineering? Well, at the end of my first year, I joined the herd and applied for a dual degree. Thanks to my not-so-stellar CGPA, I was awarded B.E. in Electrical and Electronics (EEE) as my dual and my student id code changed to B5A3.

But why did I apply for engineering when I was sure I didn't want to do it?

It was partly peer pressure and also the fact, that sticking to just MSc meant that only the academic career option was open to me. And I was not sure I was up to struggling long haul in academics. Doing Engineering meant I could sit for campus placements and get a job ( a priority for me in those days) at the end of five years.

Do I regret not taking Engineering directly and putting in an added year of studies by taking Dual? Not really. Physics with EEE was an amazing combination since the two complemented each other. I might not have been too interested in my Engineering coursework, but it did help me in getting a job that I loved. And with Physics backing me up, I did not have to face the horrors of coding after getting that job!

*Note: I realised the terms Discipline and course can get confusing for Non-BITSians. Discipline was the stream you entered, B.E. or MSc. A course was the subject you did, like Engineering Drawing, or Nuclear Physics. Each course had credits and a minimum number of credits was mandatory for each semester.*

Students in BITS Pilani came from all over the country, and staying in the hostel was mandatory. However, a few students ( about 10/12) in each batch were non-residential day scholars. Called DaySci in BITSian slang, these day scholars were usually children of the faculty/staff of BITS Pilani. Though most of the day scholars kept to themselves, I was lucky to count quite a few of them as my friends. They welcomed me into their homes, their families becoming my surrogate families. I attended weddings of their siblings, singing and dancing as if I was a family member. I played Holi with them, gorging on delicious gujiyas made by their mothers.

One of them became such a close friend, that once when I had too much laundry to wash, I took my laundry bag to her home and used the family's washing machine. When I went back to campus for my placement interviews during my practice school and didn't have a room in the hostel, I directly reached her home. Certain that she and her mother would feed me and give me a bed to sleep in!

My DaySci friends opened their hearts and home to me, giving me home-cooked meals and a place to be myself. A place to rest and get my bearings when homesickness got the better of me. So, to all my DaySci friends, thank you for making my years in BITS Pilani easy with your warmth and openness.

WASH

# CHAPTER FIVE

# EXTREME WEATHER

If you were in the habit of listening to the weather report on Doordarshan, you would have heard the name Churu. Churu was a place that was as famous in summers (for being the hottest place in India) as in winters (for being the coldest). The hamlet of Pilani, where the campus of BITS is located, is hardly 100 kilometres from Churu. Thus, like Churu, Pilani too faced extreme weather. The winters were freezing with the temperatures dipping below 0 degrees, while the summers were burning hot with temperatures shooting past 45 degrees. Living in hostels meant no amenities like heaters to ward off the cold or ACs/coolers to keep the heat away.

The extremely cold winters would also bring in the fog. For our January-May semester, the registration used to take place at the end of winter break, on the 5th of January. To reach on time, we had to factor in the delay caused by fog, as trains used to be delayed by many hours due to fog. The onward journey, between Delhi and Pilani by road, especially in dark would also turn treacherous.

In winters, to keep out the cold, our balcony doors and windows would be shut tight, and most of us would be found snuggled in our razai's post at 8 PM. 8 AM classes were usually missed as it used to be a struggle to leave the cocoon of a warm bed. There used to be a scramble in the girls' hostel to get the hot water from the geyser since the solar heaters would heat water only by noon( and that too, not very hot). Winters used to be easier in the girl's hostel than in the boys' since their room corridors opened outwards, exposing them to the elements. Plus, they only had solar heaters in their bathrooms. There used to be a running challenge in the boys' hostel as to the number of days one could go without a bath during winters!

The extreme cold did have some advantages. I personally, was happy to face winters again after braving two years of Chennai heat. I enjoyed showing off the pullovers mother had handknitted in Dehradun before our family's relocation to Chennai. Pullovers that I had had no chance to wear before. Winters also brought the joy of soaking in the sun at Sky Lawns or sometimes on the tiny balconies of our rooms.

Pilani summers were much more difficult for me to bear. The sun used to be burning hot, and even at night, our rooms used to feel like furnaces. Pilani summers meant drinking endless glasses of shikanji to quench one's thirst. Pilani was also where my friend from Latur taught me the trick of eating onions to beat the hot loo of April.

One trick that was very popular to cool our rooms was to drench the walls and the floor of the room with water. The logic behind this was the scientific principle that evaporation absorbs heat. Thus technically, when the water from the walls and floor evaporates, the room should cool down. Of course, it was only belatedly realised that this also increased the humidity, making the room feel even hotter.

Thankfully, our summer break would usually start by the middle of May. With great relief, we would board the train home, knowing that when we would return in August, the summers would have been replaced with monsoons (and pucchis). But then, that is a story for another day!

# CHAPTER SIX

# FRESHERS AND FUNDU

It was the first day in BITS Pilani, and my roommate and I had just finished unpacking when there was a knock at the door. Two second-year seniors entered and said, "Freshie intro!" My roommate and I looked blankly at each other and then at the seniors. We realised this was our first ragging session.

Frankly, the term ragging had never entered my mind. But, was there any college in the nineties in India where freshers were not ragged? Plus, remember the fact that I knew zero about BITS Pilani? I had no clue what I was supposed to say for my intro. Anyway, the seniors, who had come to rag only because they were bored, were kind enough to explain the pointers of a BITSian fresher intro.

When a senior demanded, "*Freshie intro!*" you were supposed to introduce yourself in the following format. Your name, your Bitsian id, your school, your school senior, your id senior and your hobbies. My freshie intro went something like this "Hi, my name is Harshita Nanda, my id is 1997B5164, I studied in Sishya, Chennai. My school senior is XXX, and my id senior is YYY. My hobbies are reading and music". Yes, my hobbies sound bland, but they were the safest ones since if you gave an out-of-the-box hobby you might have to prove it to the seniors. As it is, a couple of them object to my accent (go figure!).

BITS Pilani had the unofficial fresher period of about a month. For the duration of the fresher period, we girls were allowed to wear only salwar-kameez and boys were supposed to wear formal shirts and trousers to classes. I had taken only two sets of salwar kameez( at that time, I was comfortable wearing only jeans). Thus, poor me had to keep washing and interchanging between the two pairs. We freshers could also be stopped anywhere/anytime by the seniors for an intro. Plus, C'not was totally out of bounds.

The culmination of the fresher month was the freshers' lunch. My friends and I had looked forward to the fresher's lunch since that would mark the end of our fresher period. Plus, we had heard from our seniors that it was a lot of fun. For fresher's lunch, the first-year batch(boys and girls) would be divided into groups. These groups would then be sent to different Bhawans(hostels).

The dress code for fresher lunch for girls used to be a saree. Most of my friends and I spent the night before the freshers' lunch trying to arrange/borrow sarees from seniors. There was a buzz in the hostel early the next morning as we excitedly got ready, helping each other with the draping of sarees and accessories. Now, when I look at the pictures of me and my friends taken just before the lunch, I almost laugh at our expressions. We are all looking so proud, imagining ourselves to be oh-so-sophisticated. When in truth, we were just wet behind the ears eighteen-year-olds pretending to be grown-up.

Around noon, I walked down with the group allotted to me to the boy's hostel, where we were supposed to have our final ragging session followed by lunch. Our group had just been seated in the common room when there was a slight commotion. Suddenly, we were all told to leave and go back to Meera Bhawan. Fresher's Lunch had been cancelled!

The funny bit was, that the excess food made in the boys' hostels for the fresher lunch, was sent to the Meera Bhawan mess on mule carts. My friends and I were outwardly relieved but secretly disappointed at the cancellation of this rite.

There was no official fresher's lunch but our batch did graduate from freshers to first-years. That evening, my friends and I, clad in jeans, happily cycled into C'not to have Maggi and chai.

By the time I joined BITS Pilani, the GOI had started a strict crackdown on ragging. BITS Pilani admin also became very vigilant against it. This was the reason why our fresher lunch had been cancelled. Our batch was the last batch where fresher lunch was even mentioned. As I went into my senior years, the only ragging I did was asking "Freshie Intro!" to juniors. By the time I reached my fourth year, I had stopped doing that also. For all practical purposes, ragging for freshers in BITS Pilani was dead.

*Disclaimer: Ragging for girls versus the boys was different and tamer. The boys might have faced more ragging (like ransacking of rooms), but I am only talking about my perspective in the book.*

You cannot talk about BITSian slang and not talk about the term *Fundu*. Fundu was an all-encompassing word used to express how nerdy/awesome someone or something is. It could be used to describe a scientific or an academic process. Or to express one's awe of the other person's thought process. For example, one might use Fundu when one cracked a difficult theorem or if one managed to bag the most coveted company during placements. Fundu could also be used snarkily as an expression of envy when one's roommate made a GPA of ten (true story, not!). Or to honestly describe an intelligent person when you ran out of adjectives to express your admiration.

For instance, a BITSian reader of this book might use the phrase, "*Fundu ra babu!*" to express awe at the fact that I have chosen the herculean task of writing A2Z of BITSPilani!

∞
= u ∫ n d/u
INTRO!

# CHAPTER SEVEN

# GATECALLS, GHOTING AND GHOSTS

BITS Pilani hostels were strictly segregated by sex. It was prohibited for members of the opposite sex to enter the hostel, except for specific events like Fresher lunches and "Bhawan Nights". So how did a boy come a calling on a girl in the pre-mobile era?

Well, through a gate call!

He would walk up the chowkidar guarding the Meera Bhawan gate and tell him the name and room number of the girl he wished to meet. The watchman would switch on the mike, clear his throat, and after the crackle of static subsided, would announce the name and the room number. This would be broadcast to all the wings of the hostel through loudspeakers. Every girl in the hostel would come to know which girl received the gate call. Gate calls led to loads of good-natured ribbing and conjecture about whether the boy and girl were walking down the romantic pathways. Even if the gate call was strictly platonic, the conjectures would fly fast and swift.

Sometimes, if the boy was lucky, he would find kind-hearted friends to let the girl know he was waiting at the gate. Thus evading the gossip, speculation and ribbing!

If the situation was reversed, and a girl had to give a gate call, then it used to be a problem. There was no helpful chowkidar guarding the gates to announce in the mike. Thus, the poor girl had to wait till an unsuspecting chap passed by. She would then request/cajole the fellow into going to the boy's room and pass on her message. It used to be even more difficult in winter evenings when everyone would be hunkered down in their rooms.

Gate calls were a sure-shot way of announcing one's interest, as well as fueling gossip. And I do pity the modern generation for having missed out on the fun of Gate Calls. As for me, my memories of the early days of romance are all tied up with the sonorous voice of the chowkidar announcing, "Room number 715, gate call!"

Another term with "G" that is permanently etched in a BITSian's memory is **Ghoting** (verb)/**Ghotu** (noun).

Derived from Hindi, Ghoting was BITSian slang for mugging up. Ghoting, for mere mortals like us, usually happened the night before a mid-sem or exam to evade the dreaded "D".

Ghotu used to be a person whose nose was perpetually stuck in a book. This person was responsible for skewing the bell curve for the rest of us, by making clear A's in the courses. Rather than canteen or C'not, a ghotu would be found in their room or the reference library. Their focus would be fixed firmly on the bull's eye and nothing, not even Oasis (wait for O) could dissuade them from their target. Quite often we would use "ghotu" sarcastically to dissuade the said ghotu from books. Hoping to needle them sufficiently so that at least once they slip. Much in the way of the movie 3 idiots (you know, if you are not scoring well, then make sure your friends also don't score well).

Considering most of us in Pilani were nerds in the real world, for us to call someone else a greater nerd was an irony lost to us at that time.

It was a cold winter night. The fog was so thick that one could not see one's hand in front of the face. The girls of Meera Bhawan, cosy in their razais, slumbered peacefully. The night crept by slowly. As the hour hand reached 3 AM, there was a knock on a ground floor room's door. The girl in that room was startled awake. For the knock was not on the door that opened indoors into the wing but was on the outer balcony door.

Who would climb over the railing, get into the balcony and knock on the door? That too on a cold foggy night. She sat up puzzled, mulling what to do when the knock came again. Thinking it to be a prank, she called out. There was no response, except for a few more knocks and also, a faint rattling of chains. Spooked out of her wits, the girl ran into her wing's corridor, raising a hullabaloo. One by one, her wingies woke up and crowded into her room. The girls waited, but the knocks were not repeated. Everyone was mystified by the whole episode.

The next night the girls were waiting when the knocks came again. The girls, their hearts thumping in their chests, opened the door a crack, but no one was there! Fog enveloped the block, adding to the eeriness of the whole incident. The girls were now in an uproar. The warden was informed. In the mess and in rooms, there were endless debates about who/what was causing the knocking on the door. The word ghost/paranormal entity started doing the rounds. Meera Bhawan seemed to be in the grip of mass hysteria. Most of the girls were spooked. The hostel admin decided some steps were needed to address the issue. The watchman was instructed to walk within the grounds of Meera Bhawan during the night. (Till that time, the watchman would guard the gate but not enter the premises of Meera Bhawan).

Now, you might be wondering where I was during all this hullabaloo. This incident happened in my third year, and no, I was not the girl on whose door the ghostly(or not) knock had happened. However, the room where the incident did happen was directly below mine! But thanks to the extra warm razai that my mother had given me, I slept like a bug-in-a-rug the first night when the kerfuffle happened, coming to know of it only in the morning. The next night eager to check out who/what was knocking on the door, I tried to stay awake but alas, I couldn't stop the sandman from putting me to sleep.

Once the watchman started doing the rounds within Meera Bhawan, I realised the warmth of my mother's razai couldn't help me escape this time. The tap of the watchman's stick on the brick pathways, the rattle of his keychains, and the shadow of the neem tree on the bedroom wall spooked me, keeping me awake for many nights as I imagined ghosts and things that go bump in the night!

The mystery of the knock was never solved. Was it a ghostly entity or was it, mass hysteria, influenced by dark foggy nights that gripped us?

GATE CALL
GHOTU

# CHAPTER EIGHT

# HISTORY, HOSTELS AND HOMESICKNESS

BITS Pilani is one of India's premier engineering colleges but do you know its history?

Pilani is the native hamlet of the Birla family. Like most Marwari families from Rajasthan, the family too built its fortunes in the Kolkatta. But their strong ties with Pilani continued. In 1901, Seth ShivNarainji Birla started a *pathshala* for the education of his grandsons, G.D. Birla and R.D.Birla. The pathshala gained strength by becoming first a high school, followed by an intermediate college before it was finally converted to a degree college. A Birla Education Trust was formed with all the educational entities of Pilani under it. In 1964, the Birla Institute of Technology and Science was formally incepted as an Institute with Dr G. D. Birla as the Founder Chairman.

Benefiting from the Ford Foundation Grant, BITS Pilani was developed in association with the Massachusetts Institute of Technology (MIT), USA. This became the reason why BITS Pilani's course structure and grading were similar to colleges in the US. When I joined BITS Pilani in the nineties, it enjoyed the status of a deemed university. It was later awarded to become an <u>Institute Of Emminence</u>. Many BITS Pilani graduates have become CEOs and founders of successful startups.

If you visit the Birla museum, located within the BITS Pilani campus, you can see the centuries-old *palki,* which used to carry a young G.D. Birla to the pathshala!

How can we talk about BITS Pilani and not discuss hostels, our pseudo homes for four years?

Hostels in BITS Pilani were called Bhawans. The Bhawans were named after either mythological figures or inspiring leaders. The names were Malviya (Mal), Ram, Buddh, Krishna, Shankar, Vyas, Gandhi, Vishwakarma (VK), Rana Pratap (RP), Ashok, Bhagirath and Meera Bhawan(MB). All except the last were hostels for the boys.

The hostels were allotted to the students according to their year. Thus, Krishna, Shankar, Vyas, Gandhi, Ram and Budh housed the first and second-year students. While RP, Ashok, VK and Bhagirath were for third and fourth-year students. Malviya was usually for PhD and M.E. students. All students of the same discipline in a batch were allotted the same hostel. So all the MSc Physics boys of my batch were allocated rooms in Krishna Bhawan for the first two years.

In our days, boys were allocated single rooms right from the first year. Each room had a cot, a steel almirah, a chair and a desk. The hostel common rooms used to have a TV with a cable connection and a phone for receiving calls from home( we were in the nineties, and there were no mobile phones). These hostels would be enclosed by barbed wire, with no watchman guarding the gates. The boys also did not have any curfew time. Which explained the popularity of ANC with the boys.

At the end of the academic year, just before summer break, there used to be a frenzy in the hostels. One was supposed to pack everything and empty the room. Everything would then be stored in the common rooms. When the students would come back in August for the new academic year, the possessions would have to be collected and lugged into the new room allocated. This new room would be home for the next year. There used to be much huffing, puffing and groaning as the trunks, suitcases and holdalls were carried to and fro. In Meera Bhawan, apart from the common room, each block would have one room designated for depositing luggage. One year, my best friend was unlucky as her room was designated to be the storage room. She had to wait till everyone arrived and took their luggage before she got access to her room!

The reason for every year's emptying of rooms was that the summer break was used for the maintenance and whitewashing of the rooms.

The hostels in BITS Pilani were strictly segregated. The opposite sex was not allowed on the premise except for certain exceptional events, like Bhawan Nights. Bhawan nights were like school socials, but with the blessings of the college administration. Traditionally, first-year students of a particular Bhawan used to put up a cultural show for the entertainment of second-year students and their guests. Bhawan's nights used to take place in April, just before the compres (the final exams of a semester). It was a kind of farewell from Bhawan since the second-year students would relocate to a new hostel in August. The program would be followed by a special dinner in that particular Bhawan mess.

The guests of the second-year students used to be girls. The number of *'invites'* a girl received automatically increased her popularity rating. Bhawan's nights were an opportunity for the first-year students to showcase their creativity in terms of invites and the program they arranged. It was also a sneaky way for a boy to express his interest in a girl.

Meera Bhawan also used to have a Bhawan's night. That was the only time boys were allowed inside the gate. Of course, the invite used to be checked at the gate. Here I must clarify that when I am writing about being allowed inside the premise only in a particular area was allowed. There was no way individual rooms could be accessed by the opposite sex.

Now, you dear reader must be wondering if I was popular enough to be invited for Bhawan's night. In the first year, I was lucky enough to be invited to the Vyas Bhawan night by my school senior. The fun bit was that most of my fellow first years in that Bhawan were my friends, and I had a pleasant evening. My favourite Bhawan night was, of course, a Meera Bhawan night when hubby dearest and his whole gang had been invited by me and other friends of his batch. Though the food was mediocre and there was a huge crowd, I do remember all of us having a good time!

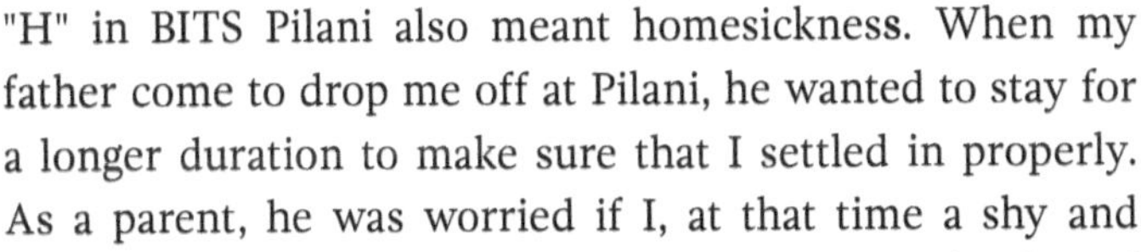

"H" in BITS Pilani also meant homesickness. When my father come to drop me off at Pilani, he wanted to stay for a longer duration to make sure that I settled in properly. As a parent, he was worried if I, at that time a shy and withdrawn girl, would be able to adjust to the hostel environment. However, much to his (and the whole family's surprise), I asked him to leave earlier than he had planned with my roommate's parents. An incident, that has gone into the repository of family anecdotes.

The reason why I asked him to leave early was that I had *wanted* to be independent, to manage everything by myself. I smugly assumed that I would never be hit by the homesickness bug that a few of my friends suffered from. I had decided to turn over a new leaf, determined not to be the girl who was so shy that she blended in the background. I sailed through my first year, savouring the newness of college. I made loads of new friends and experienced many new things.

At the end of my second year, when instead of home I spent my summer break in New Delhi, I fell prey to homesickness. "*Home*" in those days used to be in faraway Chennai, a journey of more than 40 hours. To alleviate the homesickness in the middle of the term (during Oasis or APOGEE), I started sneaking off to my uncle's house in Dehradun. Even though it was not exactly home, it offered me a familiar hug since it was the house I had spent most of my life in.

Belatedly, I realised that while being independent had its charms, managing everything on my own got exhausting after some time. One would long for the comforts of home when down with fever. Or when the mess food made your stomach grumble in annoyance. Or when the laundry would pile up, leaving you with no option but to do it yourself. Or when you had to put in an all-nighter to study, and you had to make do with the watery tea of the night mess, imagining it to be mummy ke haath ki chai.

I would never get back the "*home*" I had before I left for college. Yes, home is still where my parents live and where

I feel safe. But after I went to BITS Pilani there was a shift. I had changed, my family had changed, and the dynamics had also changed. Whenever I told my parents about my life in BITS Pilani, I would gloss over the difficulties, focussing on the fun bits. And I knew the same was true for them as well. They hid many things from me, not wanting to trouble me in a place where they knew they couldn't help me physically. When I went back home for vacations, I realised that the time I spent at home with family was momentary. It would not last forever. After the holidays, I would have to go back to the spartan hostel room.

I was now, no longer a diffident young girl but a young woman responsible for herself.

UME

# CHAPTER NINE

# INSTI, IC AND IPC

BITS Pilani has a sprawling green campus. And lording over it all is the majestic academic block that we BITSian's called Insti (short for Insititute). The Insti was divided into three blocks, FDI, FDII and FDIII. These had classrooms, labs, and chambers for the professors. FDII and FDIII were connected by corridors, while FDI was a separate block. Next to FDI was the workshop as a separate block. Some of the classrooms were huge, with theatre-like seating. These were usually for professors who had a large fan following. Whereas others were reminiscent of school days with wooden desks, chairs and blackboards.

At the centre of the Insti was our imposing Auditorium (Audi). And on its roof, lording over the whole campus, was the imposing clock tower. The architectural style of the Insti was influenced by Rajasthan with long corridors, pillared columns and ornate arches. The parapets of the first floor had jaali work, and their tops were thick ledges, perfect for perching and watching the world. The thick walls with flagged stone floors kept the Insti cool even in burning summers. Between the different wings were quaint courtyards full of shrubberies, trees and chirping birds.

The Insti was the backbone of BITS Pilani. We attended classes, studied in the library, paced the corridors waiting for the placement lists, and bit our nails waiting outside Dean's offices waiting to be handed a project. Our whole day would be spent in the Insti.

Insti was also where we bunked classes to go to IC.

IC was the institute cafeteria, whose memories of samosas and bread pakoras can even after twenty-five years, make me drool.

Situated just behind the Audi, I discovered the joys of IC only in my second year. I used to pop down there almost once daily (if not more), either alone (usually) or with friends to have tea or snacks. The IC was a saviour when there would be pongal for breakfast in the mess (every Tuesday!), and I would satisfy my hunger pangs with samosa or a bread pakora. IC used to work round the clock during Oasis, but (I think) on regular days would be open only until 5 PM in the evenings.

IC was not the most hygienic of places. Its floors were grimy, the waiter bhaiya's personal hygiene questionable, the chutneys testing our ability to dodge diarrhoea after eating them.

And yet, I miss IC.

I miss sitting in the IC alone, between 9 and 10 in the morning, just before physics CDC classes, drinking tea as I revised my notes of the previous day. I miss calling my friends cheapskates for giving a treat in IC rather than the more expensive C'not. I miss hopping into IC to while away the time when there was only an hour's break between classes, and it would be too hot to cycle back to the room.

Most of all, I miss IC ke bread pakora!

IPC or Information Processing Centre was the fancy name for BITS Pilani's computer lab. Personal computers were still a luxury in the years when I was a student at BITS Pilani. To provide BITS Pilani students access to computers the management had established IPC. This was a room full of workstations for us to practice computer coding(for CPI and CPII) and for project work for other courses. The exam for our Computer Programming course (CPII), in the second year, used to be online. Since IPC used to be air-conditioned, it was a good place to while away hot summer afternoons.

For a person who had never done computers or coding before in school, IPC initially used to be a scary place for me. Later I realised I would not be able to escape the clutches and started frequenting it more often. IPC was the first place where I coded, ran programs and learnt debugging. We all were allocated our BITSian email ids, though access to chat rooms or Yahoo (yes, Yahoo! was alive and rocking at that time) was restricted. Thanks to the BITSian email id, I could keep in touch with hubby dearest (then boyfriend) through emails, when he started his professional career in far away Hyderabad.

Initially, it used to be easy to get a desk to work in the IPC since we didn't have a lot of courses that demanded software projects. From the third year onwards, it started getting difficult since the strength of the batches had also increased. If there were no empty workstations, we used to check if any of our friends were working. We would then try to "reserve" the desk. Failing that, we would give up in frustration and try our luck later.

The admin, realising that the number of workstations was not sufficient, created another add-on room for a bigger IPC. However, by that time I was already in my fourth year and went to the IPC only for checking emails. By that time, quite a few BITSians had started getting their desktops to Pilani (laptops were still some years off). This was used for their coding projects and typing project reports. However, there was still no internet provided in the hostel rooms. So, they did need to go to the IPC for uploading etc. and good old floppies were used for that purpose.

Now, of course, even the hostels of BITS Pilani have high-speed internet, so I wonder about the fate of those rooms where IPC used to be.

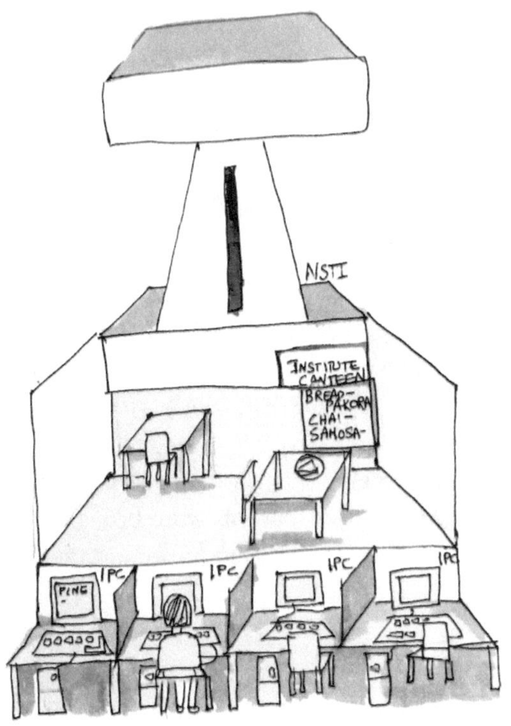

NSTI
INSTITUTE CANTEEN
BREAD-PAKORA
CHAI-
SAMOSA-
PING
IPC
IPC
IPC
IPC

# CHAPTER TEN

# JHANKAAR

To tell you the truth, dear reader, I was stumped about this alphabet. The only word I could think of, starting with "J" was junta, the BITSian slang for people/crowd. However, as I started writing the rough drafts lightning struck as I remembered this word. I couldn't help but smile, remembering memories that this word brought.

Jhankaar, a place that played an important role in our love story!

This was the late nineties. There was no music streaming platform in those days. Audio Cds had yet to make a splash. Even having one's music system used to be a big deal, and buying cassettes used to be an expensive proposition. Enter Jhankaar.

Jhankaar was the audio cassette lending library of BITS Pilani. The walls of Jhankaar were full of racks filled with cassettes. Jhankaar was also responsible for conducting the highly popular Antakshari and Bollywood music quiz during our college festival Oasis. But how did Jhankaar get a starring role in our love story?

Remember "B" for BSL? Well, BSL was located right next to Jhankaar. And guess who was the secretary of Jhankaar when I was busy playing librarian in BSL? Hubby dearest!

The physical proximity of Jhankaar and BSL helped in bringing our hearts closer! What started with casual conversations discussing our common ISC background slowly turned into attraction. By a little bit of deft manoeuvring, we would try to coordinate our shift timings, giving us time to engage in conversation and know each other better. Being the secretary meant he could take a few advantages. He would serenade me with music that I preferred when we would be on our shifts. Even after so many years, he has continued this habit of playing music to put me in a good mood.

With the winds of change bringing a transformation in BITSPilani, I sometimes wonder what happened to all those cassettes and Jhankaar.

BGL
JHANKAR

# CHAPTER ELEVEN

# KIRAN DIDI

It was almost eleven at night, and my roomie and I were almost asleep when there was a knock on the door. It was a day scholar friend. She was spending the night in another friend's room for ghoting since they both had a make-up exam the next day. Unfortunately, the friend in whose room she was staying had fallen ill. We tried giving medicines from our first aid boxes, but nothing worked. Finally, at about 12:30 AM, I knocked on the door of Kiran Didi. Kiran Didi was the caretaker/supervisor of Meera Bhawan (the girl's hostel). Kiran didi checked my friend and seeing her condition, decided to take my friend to Sarvi (Sarvjanik hospital). Thus, at 2 AM, me, my friend and Kiran didi bounced along the roads of Pilani to reach the hospital, where my friend was admitted. This incident happened in my first year, and I had almost forgotten about Kiran didi until a BITSian senior reminded me of her again a couple of days ago.

Kiran Didi used to live in the corner rooms on the ground floor of the old block of Meera Bhawan. Tall and fair, she always dressed in sarees and used to have ringlets to frame her face, quite like the movie stars of the seventies. Though many rumours about her and her marital status etc.

used to circulate in the hostel, there was no one, within my circle at least who knew her personally.

Kiran didi's rooms had a telephone and an intercom. If any parent called on her number, she would announce from the intercom, and the girl would come to attend the call. I remember my father calling on that number once when he couldn't get through my block's number. I gently dissuaded him from calling again on that number since I didn't feel comfortable attending a phone call in what was evidently, Kiran didi's sitting room.

Now, when I am writing about her, I wonder what her life must have been like. Kiran Didi was always there, but she ignored us and we, her. She was not faculty like our other two hostel wardens. So we never respected her as we respected them. What would she have felt to be stuck in that place for years while the girls around her moved on to grander things?

Or maybe, I am just overimagining. Maybe Kiran didi was happy and content in her life.

IRAN

# CHAPTER TWELVE

# LACHA AND LOVE

How can I write the A2Z of BITS Pilani and not write about lacha and love?

Lacha is the BITSian slang for conversation. Lacha sessions meant staying up late with all your friends crowding your room, discussing movies and songs. Lacha was earnest one-on-one conversations with your bestie discussing affairs of the heart. There was the delight of lacha sessions after the holidays as we caught up with what everyone did during the break and munched on goodies from home. Or the sessions that took place after eleven when the ones who had gone on a date would be teased.

Lacha sessions could happen around the bright blue tables of C'not while gulping down Blue Moon's cold coffee or around the steel tables of IC as we endlessly debated topics that seem rather inconsequential now. They could take place in the mess punctuated with guffaws of laughter, or in whispers in the RefLi. Laccha sessions were how we BITSians passed our time in those pre-internet, pre-mobile days in a place that offered us limited opportunities to get up to mischief.

Lacha sessions were how we created bonds that have withstood the vagaries of time and distance.

And while I am talking about lacha can love be far behind? For it was in BITS Pilani that I fell in love. A love that had endured time, distance and challenges. A love that feels as fresh as it was years ago.

And I was not the only lucky one. Quite a few of my batchmates got married to their BITSian sweethearts and built happy lives together.

What was the reason, that so many of us fell in love on campus? Even the nerdiest of our batch, one who had a perfect score of ten, fell in love! Was it because all of us were bound within the confines of the campus with very few distractions? Or, was it just a time-honoured rite of college to fall in love?

Whatever the reason, the one thing that I will always be grateful to BITS Pilani will be for my soulmate.

# CHAPTER THIRTEEN

# MEERA BHAWAN, MESS AND MUSIC NIGHTS

The girls' hostel of BITS Pilani is called Meera Bhawan. Meera Bhawan, or MB as it is popularly called, was initially built as a single two-storied structure. The style was similar to the boys' hostel, with thick walls and stone floors. When BITS Pilani was established, only a handful of girls would be in each batch, and this building was sufficient. However, year by year, the proportion of girls started increasing. This meant that new blocks had to be constantly added to MB to accommodate the girl students.

When I joined BITS Pilani, the old block was on one side and the newer two-storied blocks on the other, with the mess in between. For our batch, most of the girls were allocated three to a room in a relatively older block. A few of us, including me, were luckier as we got a *double-seater* (i.e. two of us shared a room) in the newest block of that time. This block was the tallest (three-storey high) and right at the edge of the MB wall. In the second year, my room's balcony faced outwards, and I could see the campus road and faculty accommodations from the balcony. It offered me a glimpse of regular life. A life different from the temporary one I was living at that time. By the second year, all of us were allocated double seaters and by the third year, we all had single rooms. However, there was still a shortfall of rooms as the batch strength had increased. Thus, a newer block was built in 2002.

To guard the virtues of the girls inside, MB was surrounded by a high wall topped with barbed wire. The only entry and exit were through a gate guarded by a chowkidar (the giver of gate calls). During the day, there were no restrictions on the comings and goings of girls, but we did have a nighttime curfew of 11 PM. If any girl reached the gates of MB after 11, she was supposed to enter her name and room number, along with the reason for the delay in a register kept in the chowkidar's hut. The next day, the warden Dr Meera Banerjee, popularly called MBanks, could also call the girl to her house, right in front of MB, to demand an explanation.

This curfew might seem a little draconian, but let me remind the reader that I am writing about the late 1990s. At home in Chennai or Dehradun, being out alone in the dark was not allowed (nor was it safe). So, to be out till 11 in the night alone and not be worried about darker elements was liberating. Truth be told, after Pilani, only in Dubai have I had the freedom and safety to be out so late.

I read a couple of years back that the night curfew for MB has been scrapped. If true, then I must applaud the college administration for creating a campus safe for women. And also, to be so forward-thinking to allow women to make their own choices.

Right opposite the MB gate was a free-standing block, the mess of MB. The mess was a giant hall where we girls used to have our meals. Pilani was in northwestern India, but most students were from the south, predominantly Tamil Nadu and Andhra Pradesh. Thus, despite all the mess workers (bhaiyas as we called them) being Rajasthani, the food did have a distinctly southern flavour. Along with roti and sabzi, sambar or rasam would also definitely be on the table. Quite a few vegetables were also made in the south-Indian poriyal style with coconut. Rajasthani staples like *gatte ki curry* and *gawar ki fali* were also often on the menu. Fun fact, after BITS Pilani, I have stopped eating *gatte* ki curry. I had enough in four years to last me a lifetime!

Paneer was saved for Sunday lunches and special grub. We would get it strictly rationed to one ladle only (no rationing for the other food items). Fryums were another staple of special grub. On special grub days, instead of regular dinner, we used to get high-tea, with usually *aviyal* and curd rice on the menu. I am assuming that the management thought we needed to eat something lighter after that one ladle of pancer dish. My friends and I used to love it when we used to have bread pakora for breakfast while skipping it on the days of pongal, having breakfast in IC instead.

The mess was where I tried to learn authentic Marathi pohe from my best friend by taking permission to go into the kitchen to cook. It was an experience I never bothered to repeat. Not because she didn't cook or teach me well, but because frankly, even then, I would much rather spend my time doing anything other than cooking! A few enthusiastic girls would also bake cakes in the single OTG provided for the use of girls (usually for their boyfriends). This was another thing that I never bothered to do.

The MB mess had a shallow cement tank in front of it that used to remain empty, except for Holi. When we used to reach the mess for breakfast on Holi, the tank would have already been filled with water. One after the other, we would either dunk our friends or be dunked by them in that tank. And then the real Holi fun would start. I knew many of my batchmates who would play Holi only in MB, not venturing out of MB gates. My friends and I were made of sterner stuff and would roam the campus with our other friends smeared in the colours.

The lunch on Holi would be a special grub, you know, with one ladle of paneer and fryums. Many times, even the bhaiyas would be covered in colour while they would serve us food. The mess used to be closed for dinner on Holi, and all of us would troop down to C'not for dinner.

Though I do not think I can recall the taste of any food from the mess, except for bread pakora, there are many memories of the mess that are still strong. The long stainless steel tables laden with the big bowls of dal and sabzi; Chhotu bhaiya walking around handing rotis to the girls; The clatter of spoons on steel plates; Girls rushing in and out during lunch; Guffaws of laughter during dinner lacha sessions; Slurping watery Maggi and weak tea in the night mess before putting in an all-nighter.

Camaraderie, laughter and collective disgust at mess food!

*Note: Grub is the, rather aptly named BITSian term for food.*

Did you know that Pilani was the only place where I danced to my heart's content? And the reason for this was Music

Night!

Music night was one of the most eagerly anticipated events for me and my friends, especially in our junior years. We would dress up to the nines and spend hours debating what heels to wear, almost as if we were going to a fancy disco. In reality, we would be walking/cycling down to Audi to enjoy (or boo) the singers of the BITS Pilani music club. The singers would croon tunes in English, Hindi, Tamil and I think even Telegu from the stage of the Audi.

While some students would enjoy the music from the seats, most of us would usually be found in the narrow space between the stage and the seats, which would have been converted into an improvised dance floor. We would be dancing our hearts out in that space. The lights would also be quite dim (thank you, department of lights) which made sure that no one could see us and hence comment on how good (or bad) our dance moves were. There was a certain freedom in just letting our hair down and just be!

The added advantage, of course, would be that there was no 11 O'clock curfew for girls on Music nights. So if we were not happy with the songs, we could always hang around having lacha on the lawns in front of the Audi.

So, to cut a long story short, music night was the BITSian version of a disco!

# CHAPTER FOURTEEN

# Normalised Ranking, Nutan and Neem Flowers

I got admission to BITS Pilani thanks to my grade 12 PCM percentage. I was from the ISC board. My fellow lunatic B5-by-choice roommate was from the Tamil Nadu State Board, while my day scholar friend was from the CBSE board.

So, how did the BITS Pilani admissions office judge all three of us, considering different boards had different difficulty levels?

To adjudge all the applicants without bias and to level the playing field, the BITS Pilani would "normalize' our marks.

The topper's PCM+English marks for a particular board were considered 100%. The percentage for the rest of the applying students was then calculated based on that. For instance, if the topper of the ISC board had a score of 383/

400, then 380 would be taken as 100%. Another student from the ISC board with a score of 375 would then have their score converted as (375/380)*100=98.66 percentile. Similar calculations were done for all the students with their board toppers. The whole list was then collated to create the normalised rank of a student. The normalized rank determined the discipline of the student. The higher the rank, the more the chances of getting a stream of your choice.

In theory, the concept of normalised ranking was good, but it did have a bias towards the state boards that were easier to score. More students from these boards would get a better rank compared to tougher boards like CBSE or ISC. This was one of the underlying reasons why students from Tamil Nadu and Andhra state boards always had a higher batch strength compared to other boards. This flaw was highlighted when in one of the junior batches, more than 500 students (out of 800) selected were from the Andhra state board.

To plug the loopholes in the admission policy BITSAT was finally introduced in 2005.

In BITS Pilani, our world was enclosed within the walls of our campus. But every once in a while, we would venture out to Nutan. Nutan was the name given to the bazaar just outside BITS Pilani gates. This bazaar was like any other bazaar found in a small hamlet of North India, complete with garbage and masticating cows. The shops sold predominantly local products catering to the needs of the local Pilani population. But why did we, the students, go to Nutan?

Well, partly to buy the things not available at Mittal stores at C'not, plus the two rather seedy beauty parlours of Pilani were in Nutan. The reason why the boys went to Nutan was, of course, the theka of Pilani was there.

The Pilani bus stand was also located in Nutan. Buses of Rajasthan state transport corporation, as well as, private companies (like Choudhary travels), would ply from there to Delhi, Jaipur and other towns. If one was adventurous or wanted to avoid the hoi-polloi that made up the travellers in the buses, one could also hire Sumos or Jeeps for their journey. I remember going to a friend's house in Chirawa in an open jeep from Nutan. The drivers of these jeeps charged per passenger, and you did need to keep your eyes shut to avoid your BP from rising at the way they drove!

Pilani falls in the district of Jhunjhunu in the desert state of Rajasthan. Contrary to our imagination of a desert, Pilani is not a desolate sandy barren piece of land. The campus, in particular, was a verdant oasis with rolling lawns in front of the Insti and native trees flanking the avenues. Throughout the year, these avenues were green and shady keeping the campus cooler than the lands outside. But the trees were also deadly, as they were home to hundreds of birds, mainly crows. Birds, that had the propensity to drop their "blessings" when one was cycling underneath the green canopy.

One tree that abounded in these avenues was the Neem. Come the month of April, the Neem trees would burst into tiny white flowers. Walking or cycling under these flowering Neem trees, one would inhale their honey/pungent aroma. An aroma, that became embedded in my senses. I didn't know how much I missed it until I smelt it again, thousands of kilometres away in a parking lot of a supermarket in Dubai. As that familiar aroma tickled my senses, I was transported back to the summers of Pilani. Of simpler times, when, my only worries would be my upcoming exams or grades. When I was carefree enough to be satisfied with a plate of Maggi and a loaf of bread with my friends. Of that first blush of romance.

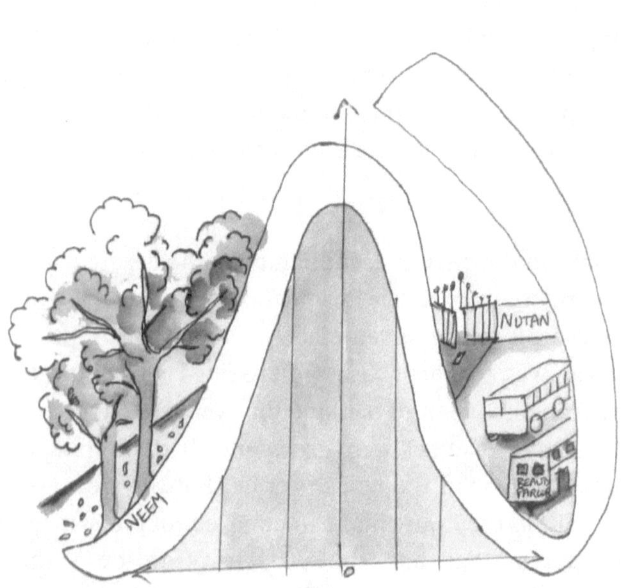

# CHAPTER FIFTEEN

# OASIS

OASIS! Even thinking about this word brings a smile to my face.

BITS Pilani was pretty isolated, and our lives were bound within the campus. Pilani's distance from New Delhi and other big cities meant there was hardly any interaction with other college students. Except during OASIS, the cultural festival of BITS Pilani.

Before I get into the details of OASIS let me give a background about the clubs and departments of BITS Pilani. The departments and clubs of BITS Pilani were quite active, with almost no interference from the faculty or college administration. The coolest departments used to be the Department of Lights and the Department of Sounds. For these two departments, first-year students were hand-picked by the senior members of the departments, and I don't think a girl was ever picked for them. These two departments were the desi version of frat boys.

There was, of course, the Department of Sponsorship and Marketing( Sponz), responsible for getting the sponsors and the money needed to run the festivals. The Department of Controlz would handle all the events of BITS Pilani. Department of RecNAcc would arrange for accommodation of Outsti students (Outsti = Outstation) who would come for the events. Creatively inclined students would join ArtND. DOPY was the name given to the Department of Photography. Apart from the departments, there were clubs. The music club, English Press Club (EPC), Hindi Press Club (HPC), English Drama Club (EDC), Hindi Drama Club(HDC), the astronomy club, the dance club and of course, Jhankaar.

Induction into a particular club/department would take place in the first year itself. A student would go higher in the hierarchy of the club/department as they became more senior. The senior-most position in a department was called Stuccan (StuCCA: Student Council of Cultural Activities).

I was not a member of any of the clubs or departments in the first year. One of the reasons was, of course, that I was unaware of them and how to join. Usually, your school or city senior introduced or guided you about it. They would mostly induct you into the club/department that they were a part of. I did not have that luxury as my school senior was also not a member of any department. I also did not have any interests or hobbies apart from reading. Thus, departments like DOPY or ARTnD were ruled out for me.

I was interested in drama and writing, but the English language drama and press club groups felt quite snotty to me, while Hindi was a language, I was not very confident in. I did join Hindi Drama Club in my second year and Hindi Press Club in my third, but mainly because my friends were members. So I used to tag along more for the company than actual serious work!

Now coming back to OASIS. OASIS takes place every October. Teams from DU and other north Indian colleges would hop into Pilani for the various competitions. BITS

Pilani, being an engineering college, was full of nerds. Thus these students, especially those from DU, felt very hip and worldly-wise to us.

Since OASIS was the showcase of BITS Pilani, all the student clubs and departments would swing into action weeks before the actual event.

Department of Lights and Department of Sounds used to handle all the technicalities for all the events in Audi. ArtND would be responsible for the posters and would erect a mammoth structure on the D-lawns in front of Audi for OASIS. This structure used to be a talking point, with all the BITSians having an opinion about it, and a picture in front of it. Members of DOPY would walk around with cameras slung around their necks, clicking pictures that were delivered to our rooms after a few days. These matte-finish pictures bring a wave of nostalgia when we see them now. Jhankaar would organise the highly popular antakshari and the music quiz that used to take place in the QT. EPC and HPC would publish news sheets during OASIS. I became a member of HPC for one of the OASIS since the secretary of the club was a friend. For the first time in my life, I even wrote an article for it in Hindi.

Most of the action for OASIS would take place in Audi. Amongst all the events, the most popular ones were the Fashion Parade (called FashP) and music concerts. I remember the rigorous auditions that used to take place for selecting the participants for FashP. A selection for the FashP team used to mean one would finally enter the hallowed club of cool people. Again, our desi version of fraternity, though this was co-ed. It also meant heartache if one auditioned and was not selected. The norm used to be for third-year girls to audition for FashP. I remember, from the middle of August, the topic of each lacha session in MB would be who was auditioning etc. Of course, yours truly had neither interest nor talent for it. I used to be more interested in the band that would headline OASIS.

OASIS was where I attended a music concert for the first time. I was introduced to the indie rock bands Silk Route, Indian Ocean and Parikrama through OASIS. Needless to say, I became fans of them for life, especially Indian Ocean. The Silk Route concert is one of my most cherished memory of OASIS since it was my first formal date with hubby dearest.

OASIS was the time when BITSians would let down their hair and have fun. During OASIS, our classes would be suspended, and the curfew for MB would be scrapped. One could even stay out the whole night if one wanted to.

The late-night lacha sessions, shivering in the cold October nights under the falling dew and sipping hot chai discussing FashP or the music concert, are memories of OASIS one cannot erase!

OASIS

# CHAPTER SIXTEEN

# PRACTICE SCHOOL, PLACEMENTS AND PCA

What else will "P" stand for in BITS Pilani if not Practice School and Placements?

Most engineering colleges offer an internship to their students. In BITS Pilani, these internships are called Practice School, and a separate department, headed by a Dean, handles the formalities for students. BITS Pilani has a tie-up with many companies where students can apply. Two semesters of Practice School are a mandatory part of the curriculum.

Practice School I (PSI) was done at the end of the second year, just before the third-year CDCs. The duration of PSI was six weeks and was done during the summer vacation. PSI was just dipping the toes to get a feel of working in an official environment. Most of the companies for PSI in our times used to be PSUs or Government labs like NPL (New Delhi), NISTADS (New Delhi), NCRA (Pune), and NIO (Goa). PSI was a graded course, and the student was supposed to submit a report for grading.

I did my PSI at National Physical Laboratory, New Delhi and learnt way more about humidity than I needed(or wanted) to know. At the end of the term, I had to defend my PSI report in a formal interview with the research scientist under whom I was working. Though I might not have learnt much technically, I did learn how to use MS Word while making my PSI (no, I seriously didn't know how to use it before PSI)! NPL was one of the few organisations that gave a stipend for PSI, and this stipend was officially my first salary.

PSII used to be one of the most critical semesters. A student had a choice of taking PSII either in the first or the second semester. This selection would determine which semester the student would appear for campus interviews. $1^{st}$ sem PS would mean $2^{nd}$ sem placement and vice-versa.

For students doing a dual-degree course (like me), the option was a one-semester thesis on campus and one semester PS, or a double sem PS ( PS for both semesters). For PSII, most students received a stipend that varied from company to company. The companies for PSII were dominated by the private and software industry. PSII was once again where your CGPA and discipline again made a difference. The better your CGPA, the more your chances of getting the company you wanted. Including the most coveted PS in France that a couple of friends were lucky to score for double sem PS.

I did my double-sem PS in a company called Tata Elxsi in Bangalore. Doing double sem PS turned out to be a boon. The management of TATA Elxsi, pleased with my work, offered me a job that I happily and gratefully accepted.

99% chances were that one would make an "A" in PS, thus making the GPA 10. This would give a huge boost in improving the CGPA. This was one of the reasons many of my fellow dualites also picked double sem PS.

Practice School gave us a good grounding in working professionally. PSII made a student realise how it is working within a professional setup. One became part of teams and responsible (to a certain extent) for deliverables.

Placements are the most important part of an engineering college. Countless times one reads the news of how a student scored a package worth crores during placements. It is this bottom line, the quality and percentage of placement, that separates the wheat and chaff of engineering colleges.

Placements would happen in BITS Pilani twice a year. Depending upon which semester PS the student had taken would determine which semester the student would appear for campus placements. Traditionally, the students would prefer the first-semester placement (August-December) as more (and better) companies would come during that time. Students like me, who had taken double sem PS, could go back to Pilani for about 10 days in the second semester during the placements.

The companies in our times used to be the usual suspects, like Infosys, HCL, Patni computers, etc. but there were certain companies like Schlumberger and Halliburton too. Companies that were highly coveted, but alas, recruited only one or two students per batch. Few companies used to fall on the typical logical/reasoning/ analytical test before selecting the candidates for interviews, while others used to be more discerning and have strict criteria of discipline and CGPA cutoffs for students.

A student's campus placement was their stepping stone in their professional careers. Placements not only depended upon how good one was in their field but also required luck to be on your side. Placement time on campus used to be nerve-wracking. And yet, it was also a time of great highs. On one hand, one would commiserate with friends who didn't make the cut trying to boost their spirits, and on the other hand, demand expensive treats in C'not from those who managed to get placed.

I remember the days of doubt and struggle hubby dearest faced while his friends got placed one after the other. And the intense jubilation when he finally got an offer after rigorous rounds of interviews. A placement that eventually led to our leaving our country behind. A couple of years later, I was in the same boat when I failed to make the cut during campus placements. It was only due to double sem PS that I had a job in hand at the time of passing out.

Getting placed was the reward for four years of hard work and dedication.

*Disclaimer: The Practice School and Placement information given here is from the time I was in BITS Pilani. Please do check https://www.bits-pilani.ac.in/ for up-to-date information*

Pilani had students from all over India, and to retain their cultural identity, most of them joined their regional associations. Faculty from that state/region would also be part of these associations. Dehradun was my home city, but during my time in BITS Pilani, my father was posted in

Chennai. Thus, I could either join Sangam, the UP/North-Indian association, or PTM, Pilani Tamil Mandaram (though I doubt PTM would have accepted me, as I was neither a Tamil nor did I know the language). Instead, I joined PCA, Punjab Cultural Association.

Unlike other regional associations, PCA did only a handful of events a year. Nor were its members close-knit. Even though it was named Punjab, predominantly Dogras of Jammu were the members. But the events PCA used to organise would be the best on campus.

PCA used to organise one dinner, where one would get authentic Punjabi food like Dal Makhani and Paneer. The dinner used to be eagerly looked forward to by members, as the quality used to be way above the regular mess food and the quantity, plentiful. PCA used to do the bhangra for Founder's Day celebrations on Basant Panchami. I remember the crowd that used to gather for the auditions of the bhangra. Needless to say, the dance always used to be a hit of the function. PCA would also do a "Lohri" function on the 13$^{th}$ of January, which used to take place in the house of a faculty member, Professor Chandhok. The whole evening, we used to sing and dance around the bonfire, chasing away the blues of Pilani winters.

But the one thing I would credit PCA the most would be introducing me to the concept of SEWA in a gurdwara. Adjoining the BITS Pilani campus was the campus for CSIR-CEERI (Central Electronics Engineering Institute). For Guru Nanak Devji's Prakash Utsav, the small Sikh/Punjabi community of CEERI and BITS Pilani would get together and organise a path plus langar. The PCA student members would enthusiastically help the day before and on the day of the langar. We would help both in cooking as well as serving the food.

Even though I was a Punjabi, before BITS Pilani, I had neither done sewa nor had ever partaken of langar. PCA was instrumental in introducing me to this beautiful part of my faith.

# CHAPTER SEVENTEEN

# QUIRKS OF BITS PILANI

For the alphabet "Q", I toyed with the idea that I would write about Quarks (those pesky sub-atomic particles) just to prove the point that I have done MSc Physics. The other option was to write about the QT, the grassy square courtyard near the Reference Library that functioned as an events venue, an open-air study, and a lacha venue. But then I realised I should write about the quirks of BITSian life.

One of the quirks of BITS Pilani was how official names were shortened, and almost everyone and everything was given a BITsian name. Thus, Meera Bhawan became MB, General Biology became GenB, food became grub, sleep became crash, etc. A few of my friends were renamed PJ, jack, JG, and Kalu. Hubby dearest's name was shortened, while mine was given to rhyme with his. Even the professors were not spared. I remember an MB farewell when in a formal speech, a student called our warden, Dr Meera Banerjee, Mbanks. And the warden was sitting right in front of her!

These nicknames and short forms stuck to us for life, becoming a part of our identity. Your fellow ex-BITSians would neither forget nor let you forget. They will still call you by your BITSian name, even after twenty-five years!

For those who are non-BITSian's and wondering what is my BITSian name? Well, the clues are there on my social media, let's see if you can decipher them!

In BITS Pilani, the responsibility of making one's timetable for a semester was with the students themselves. A list of courses available in a semester, along with the professors taking these courses, was given to the students. This was the registration booklet. On the day of registration, which would be a day before the semester formally started, the students would register under the professor that suited them the best. The students were given time slots for registration. This process was important during the first two years when everyone was doing the same courses, and also for the selection of electives. Only a limited number of students could register for a professor. Thus, those who got an earlier time slot would get the opportunity to register for the professor of their choice.

So what was the quirk?

Well, a student could, if they so desired, not attend the class of the professor they had registered for. They could instead attend classes of any other professor taking the same course. This meant that popular professors would have so many students attending their classes that there would not be sufficient seats in the classroom. I have seen, and been, one of the students sitting on the floor in such a class!

On the other hand, there would be a few professors for whom not even a single student would turn up for class. The registered professor would, of course, be the one who would correct your test/exam paper, so you did have to meet the professor at least when picking up the answer sheets. Quite an embarrassing meeting, if I can say so, from my personal experience.

The registration booklets that one received for making one's timetable also served the function of reserving seats for the classes that junta would attend. I know people who would go and reserve seats at 7 AM for a 10 AM class. Of course, you always had people who would come late and remove the so-called 'reserving' timetable on the floor. Possession, as you all know, is $9/10^{th}$ of the law!

But what was the reason that the students didn't attend the classes of their registered professors? It might be that the professor one had registered for was the only professor available at the time of registration and was a new/unknown/bad teacher. Or, and this is true, the more popular professor dropped hints in class about what questions to expect in examinations. We, being the typical Indian students, running behind grades than concepts, would pick such a professor to get help in increasing our CGPA.

But how did the students get away with attending the class of a professor under whom they were not registered? This was possible because of the biggest quirk of BITS Pilani.

No attendance!

Yes, there was no mandatory or minimum attendance in BITS Pilani. A student could choose not to attend a single class the whole semester. And yet, they could still write the exams and tests.

The no-attendance policy of BITS Pilani meant the onus was on the student to be responsible enough. But it was also one of the reasons why one could bunk the 8 AM classes in winter without feeling too guilty!

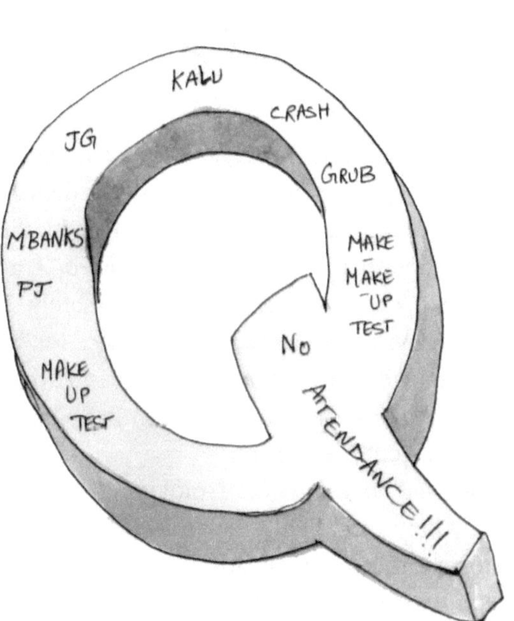

# CHAPTER EIGHTEEN

# RAF, RefLi and Redi

Pilani, the town, was no bigger than a hamlet with nothing much in the way of distractions for students to unwind. While there was a so-called movie hall in Pilani, it was just a tent with torn chairs that showed B and C-grade movies. Not a place where girls could go safely. Though I do think the boys would sometimes go there for cheap thrills. For the amusement of couch potatoes like us, who liked watching movies, the only option in BITS Pilani was RAF, Recreation Activities Forum.

RAF used to get reels of movies in both English and Hindi. Our good old dependable auditorium would transform into a movie theatre with the movie projected on a screen fixed on the stage. Stubs, as tickets for the movies, would be sold at the beginning of the semester. If one was not sure how many movies one was going to watch in a semester and skipped buying the stubs, then one could also use one's library card as a movie ticket. The library card would be taken at the auditorium entrance on the day of the movie. The charges would then be added to the student's mess bill. One then had to retrieve the library card a couple of days later from the Dean of RAF's office in FD-III. Since these RAF-screened movies were the only way one could watch movies, we tried not to miss any unless they were really, really, terrible.

For popular movies, one had to go early to bag the seats. So usually, one of the friends would finish dinner early to "reserve" good seats. And if you reached late, you might get seats right at the back, or even worse, you might have to sit on the floor in the aisle. Like how my friends and I did for the movie "Yes Boss". Whenever I catch a re-run of that movie, I remember me and my friends sitting on the floor howling with laughter at SRK's antics in that movie.

The movies shown by RAC would not be the latest, usually a couple of years old. Sometimes, even the print would not be of good quality. But it used to be a good distraction and a legit way to go on a date.

The only problem? There was no popcorn available to munch during the movie!

Befitting the status of BITS Pilani as a premier engineering college, there were two large libraries in the Insti, flanking each side of the auditorium. The main Central library was two floors filled with racks of academic books. A student could issue books from the library for reference or extra studies. The other was the Reference Library, where the published academic reports and magazines were kept. Ref li, as the reference library was popularly called, was a replica of the Central Library. But while the Central Library, due to its stack of books, was dark and musty smelling, the Ref Li was light and airy with sunlight streaming in from its row of windows.

One needed to deposit their library card to enter the Ref Li. Nor could one check out the magazines and papers from Ref Li. They were supposed to be read there. Thus, the RefLi had huge wooden desks where students used to sit and read. Below a few of the tall windows were alcoves with single desks as well. While bags were not allowed inside the Ref Li, we could carry our books inside.

Ref Li was where I spent quite a bit of my time in BITS Pilani. If we couldn't find a friend, Ref Li would be the first place we would check. The second last desk on the first floor was our group's favourite. In my first two years of BITS Pilani, most of my friends would trickle in there, one after the other, if we had a free period or were in the mood to bunk a class. While we would ostensibly sit there to study, too often, we would start talking and giggling. Ultimately, we would give up and head down to IC for some chai.

Ref Li was used as a place for serious studies, especially after the Insti hours, by people who wanted to avoid all distractions. A friend used to religiously study there every day at one of the alcove tables. She would cycle down after dinner and return just before the gates closed at 11 PM. The peace and quiet of Ref Li helped her concentrate, and I am sure her trick worked since she was a ten-pointer (one who had the perfect score of ten as CGPA). Ref Li would also double up as a dating space for ghotu couples who liked to study together (something hubby dearest and I would never be accused of).

By the start of my fourth year, I had stopped using Ref Li since the strength of the junior batches had increased. Ref Li had started being too crowded. Moreover, my friends with whom Ref Li used to be so much fun had either passed out or were on PS.

Ref Li was no fun alone.

Redi in Hindi means a hand pushcart that usually has vegetables or other items for sale. "Redi" in BITS Pilani though, was an emotion. Redi was the place for food and lacha. The bright sky blue painted redi's with a couple of wooden benches around them used to be a fixture in the front of the boys' hostels. These redi's were perfect for popping in, grabbing a bit to eat or have a lacha session while taking a break from studies. The most popular items in the redi's used to be their chai and sam chaat (samosa chaat). Nagar Ji ki redi used to be the most popular. Unfortunately, there was no redi in front of MB, and the girls had to make do with the redis of the boys' hostel. Cycling to and fro from the Insti, while crossing the boys' hostel one would find their friends sitting enjoying a snack at the redi and would be sorely tempted to join them!

R·A·F
ADMIT ONE
REFERENCE
LIBRARY
REDI

# CHAPTER NINETEEN

# Saraswati Mandir, Shiv Ganga and Sky Lawns

Directly opposite the imposing BITS Pilani clock tower, across the rolling green lawns, is the pearl of BITS Pilani, the Sharda Peeth. The Sharda Peeth is a temple dedicated to the goddess Saraswati. Sharda Peeth, or the Saraswati Mandir (as we called it), is made of gleaming white marble. Designed like the temples of ancient times, the temple has carved pillars and five shikharas. The tallest shikhara covering the inner sanctum rises to a height of 110 feet. An intricately carved marble idol of Ma Saraswati graces the inner sanctum. The temple, Dr G.D. Birla's bust in front of the auditorium and the clock tower are all symbolically designed to be in one straight line.

At first glance, the Saraswati mandir reminds one of the temples of Mount Abu, with its white marble and intricate carvings. However, as one circumambulates the temple, one realises that this temple is different. Not only does it have gods and goddesses carved on its walls, but it also has gods of science and literature, like Einstein and Tagore.

I first went to the Saraswati Mandir with friends who were Tamils. Until that time if and when I went to the temple, I would do the darshan, circumambulate the idol and leave. But these friends taught me to sit for a few moments on the temple premises before leaving. This time was used either for quiet contemplation or sometimes for socialising. While initially, I found this practice odd, later I realised I enjoyed sitting on the temple steps to re-centre myself.

Saraswati mandir visits became an integral part of my BITSian life. Before exams, placements, birthdays, or just if I felt like it, I would go to the temple. My favourite time to visit the temple used to be after 8 PM when only a few people would be there. One could sit on the cold marble steps in the dark, look at the stars, and listen to the bhajans. The atmosphere would calm and quieten your soul.

Saraswati Mandir is not the only temple in BITS Pilani. There is a small Hanuman temple as well as Shiv Ganga within the campus premises. Shiv Ganga, or ShivG, in the BITSian lingo, is a mammoth statue of Lord Shiva. The statue is placed at the centre of an island surrounded by a circular canal. There is also a small cottage on the island, used as a guest house for visiting dignitaries. There are two ghats on the banks of this canal built in the same white marble as the Saraswati temple if someone is inclined to take a dip. A white bridge is the only access to the island, and a locked gate, at the entry to the bridge kept the trespassers out. Around the circular canal is a pleasant walking track and is also a shortcut between Meera Bhawan and C'not.

Ganpati Visarjan of Maharashtra Mandal used to take place in the canal of ShivG. ShivG was also a favourite with dating couples as it offered more privacy. This fact did earn ShivG a rather notorious reputation.

The original Skylab was the first US space station that disintegrated in 1979. Skylab of BITS Pilani was a small restaurant/kiosk built in a similar shape to the original Skylab, run by Pappu Bhaiya. This Skylab was located on the lawns next to Birla Museum near FDIII. Thus, these lawns came to be known as Sky lawns or just Sky. The Sky was famous amongst the BITSians for its shikanji and sandwiches. Many winter afternoons were spent basking in the sun on sky lawns with friends. Many department and club meetings would also take place on the lawns.

My most endearing memory of Sky, however, is not of its lawns but of a classroom in FDIII.

Mathematical Models of Physics (MMP) was an MSc Physics CDC. For most of the class, this course was OHT. The professor taking this course was Dr Kulkarni ( nicknamed Aku). Realising we needed help in the subject, he decided to take extra classes. Though these classes were quite helpful, they used to be very long, stretching to almost 3 hours! Halfway through, the professor would realise that our attention had started wandering. He would then send a few of the students to get tea from Sky.

Drinking Sky's well-brewed tea and the whole class discussing the peculiarities of MMP with the professor remains one of my favourite memories.

# CHAPTER TWENTY

# TAMIL NADU EXPRESS

My story about BITS Pilani would be incomplete without even a single mention of Tamil Nadu Express.

According to Wikipedia, Tamil Nadu Express (12221/ 12622) is a superfast train between Chennai Central and New Delhi Railway stations. A distance of over two thousand kilometres is covered in a time of about 34 hours (more if it encounters the fog in winter). What Wikipedia doesn't tell us is that the Tamil Nadu express was the firm favourite of the BITSian junta from Chennai and other parts of Tamil Nadu.

At the beginning of January and August, Tamil Nadu Express from Chennai to New Delhi would be packed with BITS Pilani students, ready for their new semesters. In May and December, the same students would be coming back after writing their exams for a few weeks of reprieve. Come November, we used to fill out the concession forms, and it used to be the responsibility of the Student's Union to book our tickets from New Delhi to Chennai. For the return journey, we needed to book the tickets ourselves. For these two/three days, the only travellers in the sleeper coaches would be BITSians (AC coaches were still unaffordable and flights out of reach).

In its 2000+km journey, Tamil Nadu Express would criss-cross the length of India. It used to be fascinating to see the landscape of the country changing. The paddy fields of Tamil Nadu would give way to the sugarcane fields of Maharashtra. One could see the ramparts of Gwalior fort and once when the train was very late, I even managed to catch a glimpse of the Taj Mahal. The mannerisms of the train staff also would change whether the train was journeying northwards or south. When starting from the Delhi station coffee would be pronounced as Ko-fee, while closer to Chennai, the same person would start pronouncing it as Kaaa-pi. The same would happen for chai (it would become chaaya as we reached closer to Chennai).

There were little rituals and routines that I used to follow on this train journey. Cup O'Noodles and curd rice from the pantry car used to be my preferred dinner. A cup of Dinshaw's ice cream at Nagpur used to be a must, as well as, try and get juice from Vijaywada. However, despite all my efforts, I failed to have it even once and did almost miss my train a couple of times because of it.

The Delhi-Chennai travel in May used to be like travelling in a hot tin can. To beat the heat, we used to fill our bottles by buying ice on the platforms. And then used to curse the efficiency of Milton bottles in keeping things cold as we impatiently waited for the ice to melt so that we could drink cool water. The same train would be ice cold as we journeyed north towards New Delhi in January. Even after shutting all the windows, the cold would still seep into the compartments. There was also the added exasperation of the delay caused by fog.

Travelling in Tamil Nadu Express used to have a sense of familiarity since all fellow travellers used to be BITSians. But there was also a sense of alienation since I was the only North Indian in the group, one who didn't understand the language spoken around me. I used to sit by the window surrounded by friends and yet, kind of alone since I never had a clue about the conversation flowing around me. Moreover, I knew that since I didn't belong to any group on the train, the onward journey from New Delhi to Pilani I had to do on my own. The onward journey did become easier when hubby dearest (then boyfriend) entered the picture, but we could travel between Delhi and Pilani together only a few times.

And yet, there would be moments of camaraderie. Fellow blogger Aarthi usually used to have a relative meet her at one of the stations. If I was in the same coach as her, she always shared her homemade filter coffee and biryani with me. Another friend helped me out by getting my belongings from Pilani to Delhi when I was travelling from Pilani to Chennai for the last time.

Journeys on Tamil Nadu Express were full of difficulties. We had to brave the elements, eat food that was not really palatable, and adjust to the questionable hygiene of Indian Railways. And yet, these journeys taught me independence, to find the inner strength to handle everything by myself.

It also taught me how to be with my thoughts and enjoy my solitude.

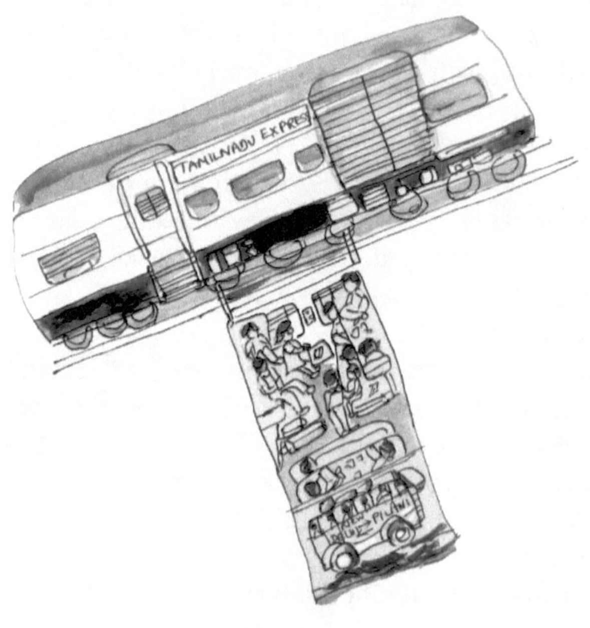
TAMILNADU EXPRESS

# CHAPTER TWENTY-ONE

# Unity In Diversity

Our country India is a melting pot of cultures, regions, religions, and languages. And a slice of it was visible in BITS Pilani as well. There were students from all over India. From Kashmir in the north to Kerala in the south, from Gujarat in the west to Bengal in the east.

Though students from a couple of states did dominate the batch strength, the other regions tried to hold on to their identity through cultural associations. I was a part of the PCA, but that did not preclude me from joining in when other associations were celebrating their festivals. Quite a few of my close friends were from Maharashtra. Thus, I became an enthusiastic participant in the Ganesh Chaturthi celebrations that the Maharastra Mandal of BITS Pilani would help organise. From the day of the sthapana of the idol to visarjan, we would be a part of each day's event. One year it was double the fun since the Ganpati was kept at my day scholar friend's house. Similarly, quite a few of my non-Punjabi friends would tag along with me for langar and Lohri celebrations.

My Odia friends taught me the importance of Saraswati Puja, while the dandiya during the Sharad Navratri was a time for fun and frolic. For Holi and Diwali, all of us would come together and celebrate these festivals.

The mess of BITS Pilani introduced me to the specialities of South Indian food that I probably would not have tried otherwise. Even if not 100% authentic, it opened my eyes to the variety of food available in India. Through my Kashmiri Pandit friends, I learned more about their exodus than a recent politically motivated film. Their stoicism and the urge to do well in life hid the pain of leaving their homeland.

The local population of Pilani was steeped in tradition. It showed me the earthiness and the raw beauty of a small hamlet in India. But it also made me aware of the importance of girl education in breaking years of patriarchal rituals. It made me realise how lucky I was to be given the advantage of education and the rural-urban divide of India.

There were a few students, like hubby dearest, who refused to join any regional association. He took advantage of the diverse states to which his friends belonged. He travelled the length and breadth of the county during holidays to visit the hometowns of his friends, discovering the beauty of our homeland.

It was not all peaches and roses, though. Being a private college, the fees of BITS Pilani are high, making it out of reach of quite a few students. Only families above a particular economic threshold can think of sending their students to BITS Pilani. This was one of the reasons why we all wanted a "good" job. A job, that would pay well. I know of friends whose parents had mortgaged their ancestral properties to be able to afford to pay the fees. In defence of BITS Pilani, they did offer generous scholarships to deserving students, but only after admission.

A few months back, I read an article about the inherent casteism in the BITS Pilani written by a former student. It is true that BITS Pilani does not have any reservations except for the BET staff. It might be my privilege speaking, but for me, rather than caste, I think there was a problem of regionalism. The students of the two states that dominated BITS Pilani did not mingle with the students from the rest of the country. While exceptions are always there, the students from these two states already had their school friends/seniors and stuck to their cliques and groups. Hence, they did not feel the need to step out of their comfort zone.

For students like me, ones who didn't belong to a particular region or state, BITS Pilani was a place to make friends from all over India!

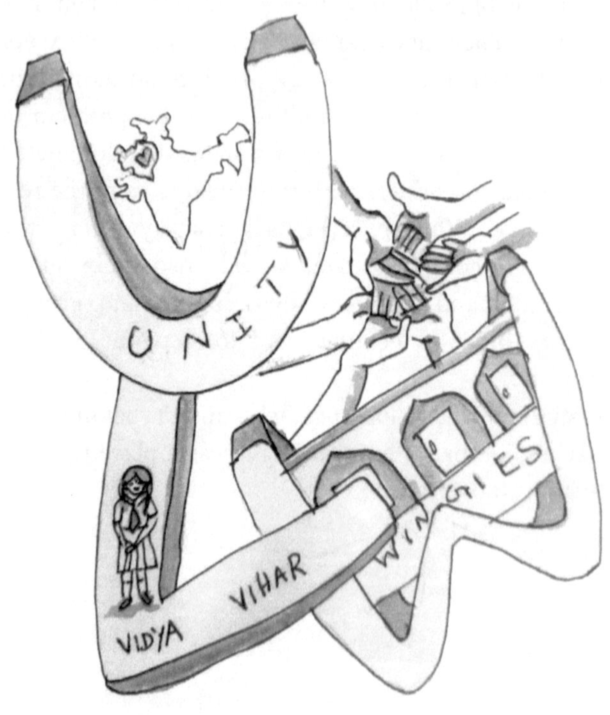
UNITY
VIDYA
VIHAR
WINGIES

# CHAPTER TWENTY-TWO

# VIDYA VIHAR AND BBVP

The small town of Pilani falls in the Junjhunu district of Rajasthan. To reach Pilani, one must first reach either Delhi or Jaipur, and then travel the further 200km journey by state transport corporation buses, through the heart of rural north India. Another alternative is the metre gauge train from Delhi's Sarai Rohilla station. This train deposits the passenger at the Loharu junction. From Loharu, it is an hour's journey by bus or jeep. Either way, your journey ends at the Nutan market bus stand right in front of the gates of Vidya Vihar, the formal name of the BITS Pilani campus.

Vidya Vihar, or the home of knowledge, is a sprawling 328-acre oasis, with Insti on one end and Sharda Peeth opposite it. Flanking the avenues between Insti and the temples were the boys' hostels. Set just behind the lane of Saraswati Mandir was the Meera Bhawan and then accommodation for faculty and staff. Apart from the hostels, faculty/staff accommodations, and academic blocks, there was also a sports complex including a swimming pool, Birla Museum and even a dairy farm, all within the Vidya Vihar campus.

Even though Vidya Vihar was in the middle of rural India, the security used to be pretty tight. Not many locals ventured inside the campus. The campus was safe enough for us girls to travel to and fro from Insti alone, even at 11 PM. Even during Oasis, when hordes of outstation students would be on campus, I never felt unsafe within Vidya Vihar.

On the left side of Insti, between the boy's hostel and Meera Bhawan, was another icon of Pilani, Birla Balika Vidya Peeth or BBVP, a residential/day all-girls school.

The BBVP and Meera Bhawan shared a wall, with the back wing of Meera Bhawan's old block overlooking the playground of BBVP. My friends who had rooms in that wing would complain about the incessant noise or music from the playfield, especially when there would be sports day or annual day practice in BBVP. Sometimes, a boarder from BBVP suffering from homesickness, who had a cousin living in Meera Bhawan would call out from the wall, adding to the irritation of BITSians trying to study.

The girl day-scholar students in BITS Pilani were ex-BBVP students whose famous alumni are the singer Neeti Mohan and her sisters. On Sunday afternoons, C'not used to be filled with the residential BBVP students who would be on a day out. Proving that whether you were a school student or an engineering student, C'not was the only place to hang out in Pilani. The residential BBVP students were only allowed to go to C'not and Saraswati Mandir, and that too with a chaperone.

BBVP also occupies a place of pride in India's history. BBVP NCC girls band has been a regular participant in India's Republic Day parade. While I was unaware of this fact in BITS Pilani, the first time I saw the girls' band marching was on TV while watching the parade in Dubai. Even though I had not had any direct interaction with BBVP while in BITS Pilani, I couldn't help but feel emotional at the Pilani connection.

# CHAPTER TWENTY-THREE

# WINGIES AND WORKSHOP

A word that is imprinted in a BITSian's mind is "wingies".

The hostels or Bhawans of BITS Pilani were huge buildings. A central staircase rose to lead to the corridors or the wings of the building. All the rooms of a particular wing shared the bathrooms/toilets. The students who had a room in your wing became your "*wingies*".

Wingies were further differentiated as "sidey", the one whose room was adjacent to your room; "Oppy", the one whose room was opposite yours ( only in new blocks of Meera Bhawan); "Backie", one whose room was behind yours, with both of you sharing the wall at the back of your room( this was in Boys' hostel as well as Meera Bhawan old block). Each wing in the new block of MB used to have twelve rooms, one on each side of the corridor. The corridor would end in BOGS at the far end and the staircase/common room at the other.

The hostel administration allotted the rooms in the first year based on discipline. From the second year onwards, it was for the students to decide with whom they should make a wing. It used to be a tough decision as your wing would be your support system. They were the ones who always had your back. It was important that even if your wingies were not your bosom buddies (though they usually were), you should at least be on good speaking terms with them. Plus, wingies needed to have good personal hygiene as bathrooms were going to be shared with them. And believe me, this second point really mattered!

In the first year, everyone was trying to adjust to a new environment. But we all got along. Groups were formed and broken, arguments flared and were pacified as we discovered each other's mannerisms, habits and nature. By the end of the year, I had made friends who became very close. For the next three years, as we shifted our rooms from block to block, they would be my wingies.

My wingies came from Kashmir, Dehradun, Baroda, Maharashtra, Chennai, and Rajasthan. Since we were from all over India, we decided to name ourselves MSMT, or the Mile Sur Mera Tumhara group, inspired by the iconic Doordarshan video that showed the beauty of India's diversity.

Wingies were the ones from whom we borrowed (or lent) dupattas, footwear and accessories. Wingies were the ones who helped in draping sarees for the official pictures or farewells. We celebrated birthdays together at twelve in the night and received (or gave) birthday bumps from our wingies. We commiserated and supported them over heartbreaks or failure to clear placement interviews. Wingies were ones with whom one had extended lacha sessions while sharing snacks sent from home. They were also the ones with whom we fought for hot water in peak winter.

And, of course, wingies were the ones with whom one shared a plate of Maggie and a loaf of bread when we wanted a break from mess food.

*BOGS: The BITSian name for bathrooms/toilets. BOGS would have two bathrooms, and two toilets, along with two stand-alone sinks, an electric geyser and a solar geyser.*

One feature that I loved about BITS Pilani was the fact, that irrespective of the discipline, one needed to complete the common courses in the first two years. Two of the most important courses in the first year were Workshop and Engineering Drawing. Both courses had a massive four credits, so a "D" in them could sink your CGPA. These two courses were an important base in our engineering education. While Engineering Drawing was not my cup of tea, Workshop was a course that I loved.

The workshop was a stand-alone block next to FDI. This massive warehouse-like structure used to hum with activity. There were lathes and machines to cut wood and areas for polishing, electroplating, etc. The workshop was a hands-on course where one was supposed to operate these machines and build things. The funny part was that while we were not given any protective gear to wear ( no gloves or goggles or coats), the workshop staff used to be very particular about their no-open-shoes policy. They would send back students if they were wearing sandals or chappals. I remember being sent back once since I was wearing sandals. I then exchanged shoes with a friend (a wingie) in the Ref Li, as I didn't want to cycle back to MB to change my footwear. I ended the semester with a silver electroplated candle stand made by myself and an "A" grade (woohoo!). Alas, how and where I lost the candle stand, I do not know.

We went back to the workshop for our second-year course, Measurement Techniques (MT). While I do not remember what I did in the workshop for MT, I do clearly remember learning how to use the Theodolite in that course! (*Theodolite is a surveying instrument used for measuring angles*)

# CHAPTER TWENTY-FOUR

# Xtras and Xerox

I decided to take a little bit of creative liberty and skip the "e" of extra as I try to explain the xtras of our mess bill.

Our mess bill was divided into two parts, basic and extra. The basic mess bill was what everyone had to pay, irrespective of what and how much they ate. It included the usual dal, roti, rice, and subji, available every day plus the ladleful of paneer for special occasions. The mess bill used to come monthly. If a semester's mess bill was not paid before the start of the new semester, the report card could be withheld. And then, there would be questions that needed to be answered at home!

Apart from the basic mess bill, there were also mess xtras. These include milk, curd, non-vegetarian food, eggs in breakfast, packs of tiger biscuits and watery Maggi. The last two used to be available in the night mess from 10:30 PM to 11:30 PM in MB. For daily items like milk and curd, we would purchase the tokens for a month. Every day we would give these tokens to the bhaiya handing out plates from behind the counter before taking these items (milk was for breakfast and curd in lunch). For extras like eggs or packs of biscuits, one needed to enter one's id in the register kept at the mess manager's table. At the end of the month, the extras would be added to the basic mess bill.

The non-food item that could also be added to the mess bill as an extra was the RAF movie tickets.

The amount of my mess xtras would decrease exponentially as the semester advanced. At the beginning of the semester, the bank account would be flush after depositing the bank draft father would give for the semester's expenses. One would feel quite rich and order xtras left, right and centre. However, by the time the semester drew to a close, one would realise the bank account running perilously low. This would mean skipping the xtras to keep the mess bill low so that one could pay the mess bill with the money remaining.

For those who are wondering why I couldn't have asked my father for more money, well I could have. And he would have sent it too. But remember, we are middle class. Money was there, but was usually tight. Somewhere at the back of my mind was always the thought that I was studying in an expensive college and thus, needed to avoid unnecessary expenses. Managing expenses in the money given for a semester also gave me a good grounding in handling finances. While the first year was tough (I remember my result being withheld due to non-payment of mess bill), I became more sensible later and a pro at juggling expenses.

In today's digital age, one can scan documents through a smartphone and email them. In those pre-smartphone days, we had to depend upon Xerox to copy notes. One needed to Xerox, if one was in the habit of regularly bunking classes (thank you, no attendance policy), if one didn't attend a good professor, or if one was genuinely lazy in taking notes. While there was a massive Xerox machine in the Insti in the FDIII block, I preferred to get my notes xeroxed within MB.

Near Kiran didi's room, was a room with a xerox machine as well as an STD/PCO booth. STD booths were how we stayed in touch with our families. We would start lining up from 10 PM and then impatiently wait to call after 11 PM when the call rates would be cheaper. This Xerox/PCO room usually had two local Pilani girls manning the desk. These girls, who did not look older than twenty, would gossip, crochet, knit and sometimes, put beautiful Mehendi for each other as they whiled away their time.

If there were too many pages to Xerox, they would snidely comment on how many classes we had bunked. They also shameless eavesdropped on our conversations (we usually never kept the PCO booth door closed as it used to get suffocating).

Like Kiran didi they were always there but usually ignored.

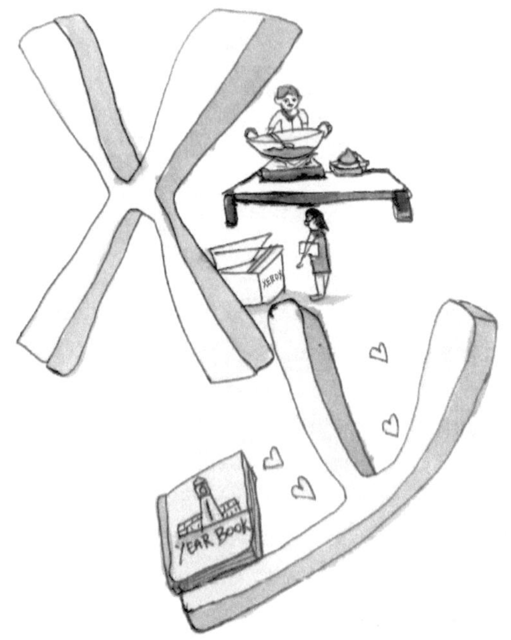
XEROX
YEAR BOOK

# CHAPTER TWENTY-FIVE

# YAMS AND YEARBOOKS

It was the first week in college. I was feeling quite hot after a long walk from the Insti at 1 PM. The daily walking to and from the Insti in the August heat was taking a toll. Not having eaten anything after breakfast at 8 in the morning, I was also quite ravenous. As I walked into the mess, I was hoping that there would be a decent vegetable curry for lunch. Though I was not a fussy eater like my other friends, I still wasn't comfortable with the food. My tastebuds were still adapting to the peculiarity called mess food.

Taking the plate from the mess bhaiya, I sank into the first available chair and ran a critical eye on the mess table. There was dal, rasam and a bowl of dry aloo sabzi. My face lit up. Aloo sabzi was my favourite, and the one in the bowl looked delicious. Roasted with cumin, its colour was a perfect golden brown. My heart did a little jig. I was finally going to lunch well. Even if the rotis were half-baked (as they usually were), the subzi would be enough to sustain me till dinner time. Picking up the serving bowl, I dumped a heap on my plate. Eagerly, I shovelled a spoonful into my mouth and immediately almost spat the whole thing out.

"This is no aloo!" Screamed my tastebuds.

As I gulped some water to wash away the taste from my mouth, looking at the mountain of that vile subzi on my plate, a senior sitting across leaned over and said, "It is yam!". Our sneaky mess cook would cook the yams in exactly the same way as potatoes to fool us. That day, I trashed food for the first time in my life. A friend did show a trick later to eat yams by dousing them in ketchup so that they kind of tasted like chips. However, my tastebuds revolted at eating that combination too.

From that day onwards, if any vegetable in the mess looked like potatoes, I would first take a trial bite before dumping the whole lot on my plate!

In BITS Pilani, every batch had its yearbook, compiled by the yearbook committee. The pattern of the yearbook used to be the same. It would be pictures of the students, details like IDs etc., and a few short lines about them. The students were organised according to their discipline. For people doing dual, like me, it was the first degree that counted. So my entry in the yearbook is with the batch I joined BITS Pilani with, not the batch I passed out ( a year later).

The short write-ups were what we had the most fun with. The whole wing would come together to create a write-up that would, on the surface, feel as if we were praising the student, but in truth, we would try to be roasting them.

A few years back, I dug out my yearbook to show it to my children. They were not impressed by the big hardbound book, full of black and white passport photos of people they had never met, and ran off to play. I was left behind, sitting on the bed, flipping through the pages.

As I read through the write-ups, I chuckled at the references to individual idiosyncrasies and hidden references to boyfriends/girlfriends. How hard we had tried to be witty and how miserably we had failed. Plus, most of us looked awkward in our passport photos. Our faces still retain traces of teenage gawkiness. Not to mention that most of us were anyway, certifiably nerds at that time.

The yearbook used to be a repository of memories. Most of us used to get our yearbooks signed by our friends and batchmates. In the hope that etching their names in the yearbook would etch that person too in our memory.

I sighed, seeing photos of friends who were once so dear to me. And whom I am now barely in touch with. I remembered the good bits, the laughter, the fun, the gossip, the teasing. When our whole lives were ahead of us, and the world waiting to be conquered by us. I don't even know how or where some of them are. Will I be able to recognise them if I bumped into them in the street? I do not know the answer. For now, my memories would have to suffice.

*My yearbook is in Dehradun, but hubby dearest has a soft copy of his yearbook in Dropbox. His copy of the yearbook was a great help in my attempt to write the A2Z of BITS Pilani.*

XEROX
YEAR BOOK

# CHAPTER TWENTY-SIX

# ZIG-ZAG PATHS

As I sat down to write for the alphabet "Z", I stared at the blank page, wondering what I should write about. In desperation, I asked my BITSian friends for an idea. Someone suggested I should write about zuk zuk one (001). The first rank holder in the normalised list. I mulled about it. 001 in our batch was the all-India CBSE topper, who left BITS Pilani after a few weeks for greener pastures of IIT. What more could I possibly write about it? Nothing! It would have been only a few lines. Another friend suggested writing about the "zzzz's of winters". Again, it would have a single line. " I bunked many classes due to zzz's in winters."

I then thought about writing about the things I had skipped, like Sarvi (Sarvjanik hospital ), and Health Centre, and the chicken pox epidemic that had struck one year. I could write about the peacocks, the creatures that everyone finds fascinating but who were pests in BITS Pilani, with their cawing at odd hours. I could also write about the tiny bugs, nicknamed "poochies", who made our lives miserable during monsoon. I could write about the horrors of make-up tests and open book exams. Or, I could write about the many success stories of the alumni of BITS Pilani. Of the alumni who became founders of start-ups, CTO's and

CEOs. Better yet, I could express my gratitude to my alma mater.

And yet, I was not very happy with the ideas. Something was missing. I kept the notebook aside for some time, deciding to re-look at my notes again.

Looking at my notes again, I was struck by the fact that my thoughts had meandered like a zig-zag. Just like my life's journey has been after passing out from BITS Pilani years ago. Just as many of my batchmates' life journey has been. So many of them quit their corporate jobs to pursue their passions. They became artists, NLP practitioners, dance teachers, poets and .... authors.

These chapters were written when I was looking back at my four years of BITS Pilani with sepia-tinted glasses. But life was not all fun and games in BITS Pilani. There were adversities, lows and heartbreaks. And yet, going to BITS Pilani was the best decision. I learned independence and resilience. The fact, that I could survive by myself, even in the toughest of circumstances.

And dear reader, the best bit? I found my soulmate there.

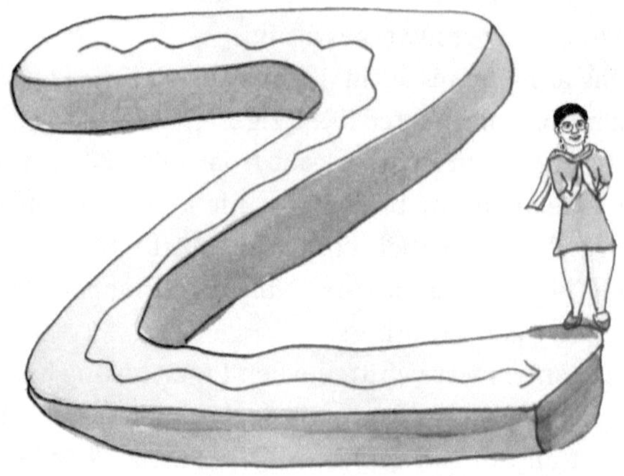

# BITSian Glossary

When two BITSians get together, they usually lapse into BITSian slang, making it difficult for non-BITSians to follow their conversation. I have tried to collate a few commonly used slang/terms, that dominate a BITSian's vocabulary.

**ANC**: All night canteen

**Audi**: Our multipurpose Auditorium

**APOGEE**: Time to sneak off for a small break, though some used to work day and night for it.

**BOGS**: Bathrooms of Graduate Students...Need I say more?

**BOSM**: The BITSian sports meet.

**Boss**: A way to call the helpers at c'not.

**C'not**: the only place to hang out in BITS Pilani, home of Blue Moon and paneer Maggi.

**Compres**: End of semester exams, where one would dream about going home.

**Crash**: The BITSians name for sleep and what the IPC computers would do if you hadn't saved your code.

**CDC**: Core Discipline Courses. What you actually joined BITS to study.

**Fundu**: A term used to describe how awesome someone/something is. It can also be used in sarcasm

**Ghot/Ghoting**: A term used for studying.

**Grub**: The food that we would get in the mess.

**Gen**: a short form of general, could be used as an answer for anything.

**God**: someone who is usually a TenP and is way better than you in almost everything.

**Guss**: Let it be (literally, not to be confused with the Beatle song).

**Hazaar**: A term to define a big number. For instance, "Hajar doubts" or "Hajar universities". I even heard this term in the movie, Chashmebudoor!

**IC**: Institute Canteen, home of the world's best bread pakora

**Insti**: Institute with classrooms, where we used to go attend classes ( no, seriously!)

**IPC**: A scary place where they made you learn computers and coding.

**Junta**: The BITSian way to refer to people. Can be one person or haazar people.

**Ju**: no not the Hindi meaning. Ju meant junior. Ju referred to a person from a lower batch usually from the same school/city etc.

Kela: Not a term to be used in polite company, Kela in simpler words meant embarressment.

**Lacha**: BITSians don't talk, they lacha.

Loci: The term was used ( and not very politely) for the local population of Pilani

**Mid-sem**: predominantly for CDCs when instead of regular tests you would have one big humungous exam in the middle of the semester.

**Make-up**: No, it doesn't mean cosmetics. It meant the test that you could take if you missed the originally scheduled one. You did need permission from the prof to be eligible to write it.

**Nite-Out**: This happened during OASIS or the day before mid-sem/compres when the sandman was kept away usually with the help of chai.

**Outsti**: Outstation, usually referred to for girl students from DU.

**Open Book**: A type of test where you could take books for exams, and yet score a Zuk.

**Psenti**: Pronounced as senti (P silent) it was the Bitsian term for sentimental. One could have psenti-sem ( ie the last semester) or go psenti (aka going steady).

**Phoda-phadi**: A sarcastic way to congratulate someone on doing well in tests/exams/CGPA.

**RefLi**: A place where people used to go to ghot and also do time-pass.

**Rod**: nope not a steel rod, but difficult.

**Sack**: opposite of rod, easy.

**Special Grub**: Food that we would get in the mess on Sundays and Festivals.

**Sarvi**: Sarvjanik hospital. Birla Charitable trust hospital for the rural population of Pilani. It was the only hospital in the whole hamlet. One avoided going there until there was no other option.

**Test Series**: The dreaded scheduled tests that used to make the first two years miserable

**TenP**: The irritating person who would score a perfect CGPA of ten and skew the bell curve for the rest of the batch.

**UVS**: Professor Usha V Subramanium, the god of CPI and CPII.

**Vela**: An integral part of BITSian lingo. Vela, derived from Hindi, in BITSian slang, meant being absolutely free. Velapanti is the verb that describes activities to occupy free time.

**Zuk**: Zero, zilch.

# About The Illustrator

Girija Hariharan is an artist and Muralist based out of Bangalore, India. She works with street art, large art installations and art intervention workshops to effect social change and community healing. Recognised as one of the top innovators of Bangalore, her street art and interviews have appeared in multiple publications. Along with traditional fine art mediums, Girija explores body art, music, poetry, tech art, graphic design, book covers, and illustrations. Her original artworks are sold worldwide, with her primary themes amalgamating feminism, mythology, anthropology, environment and spirituality.

Girija can be reached on Instagram at @2flatbrush

# About The Author

Harshita Nanda is an avid reader and a lover of the written word. An ex- 1997 batch BITSian, she became a stay-at-home mother after relocating to Dubai. The passion for the written word, however, continued to burn. Her first novella "Xanadu: Three Souls Searching For Paradise" was published in 2021. She has been part of many anthologies, including Disobedient Girls by TMYS. She was the third-place winner in Readomania's Valentine's Day short story contest and the orange flower award nominee for 2021. Her articles and short stories are regularly published on leading websites like SheThePeople.tv, Momspresso.com and WomensWeb.in.

"BITS and Pieces: A Collage Of My BITSian Memories" is her first non-fiction book.

Harshita can be reached on Twitter at @ashnhash and on Instagram at author_harshita.

# Other Titles By The Author

- Xanadu: Three Souls Searching for Their Paradise

**Anthologies**

- Disobedient Girls
- The Fiction Collective
- Life During Covid-19
- Navigating Covid-19

www.ingramcontent.com/pod-product-compliance
Lightning Source LLC
Chambersburg PA
CBHW021548150726
47990CB00006B/2447